Settle and Giggleswick

IN GIGGLESWICK CHURCH

Impressions of Settle
and Giggleswick...

I descended an exceedingly tedious and steep road, having on the right a range of rock hills, with broken, precipitous fronts. At the foot of a monstrous rock called Castleberg, that threatens destruction, lies Settle, a small town in a little vale.

Thomas Pennant (1775).

Giggleswick has long been famed as a seat of learning. We have now, though the population of the township is only about 750, three excellent masters in the Grammar School and boarders from all parts of England and even America...we have likewise a French gentleman teaching that language, a Ladies' seminary, a Dame's School, beside mine [Giggleswick National School].

William Lodge Paley (1825).

As the story of Settle unrolls, it becomes clear that the history of the town is bound up with the history of transport. The age of the green roads and the pack ponies, the age of the turnpike roads and the coaches, the age of steam and the age of petrol, have all, in their turn, influenced the structure of the town. its occupations, buildings and population.

E M Buckle (1973).

Giggleswick has changed to a far less degree than Settle. Except for the row of houses facing the Keighley and Kendal road at the top of Belle Hill, and the new School buildings and the Workhouse at the other end of the village, its streets and boundaries are much the same to-day as they were at the time of the Commonwealth.

Thomas Brayshaw and Ralph M Robinson (1932).

A POPULAR HISTORY OF
Settle and Giggleswick

by W R Mitchell

Visuals by Peter Fox

THE FOLLY

CASTLEBERG

1993

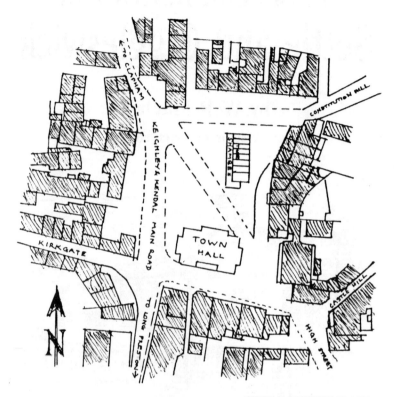

SETTLE MARKET PLACE

Published by Castleberg, 18 Yealand Avenue, Giggleswick,
Settle, North Yorkshire, BD24 0AY

Typeset in Clearface and printed by Lamberts Printers,
Station Road, Settle, North Yorkshire, BD24 9AA

ISBN: 1 871064 95 3

An Introduction

THIS story of the evolution of Settle and Giggleswick is presented in chronological order and spans the 1,926 years between two French invasions—the Norman Conquest (1066) and the arrival of peaceful emissaries from a French town, Banyuls Sur Mer, 'twinned' with Settle (1992).

In gathering together the many scattered notes relating to local history, for presentation in a narrative form, I have followed the well-established local procedure of quarrying material from Whitaker (*History of Craven*) and Messrs Robinson and Brayshaw (*The Ancient Parish of Giggleswick*).

Thomas Brayshaw's name bobs up everywhere, even on a brass plaque in the pew I occupied in Giggleswick Church for the Christmas Eve carol service, 1992.

The book includes information gleaned from a host of Settlers and Giggleswickians, some of it during the course of local history courses I conducted under the auspices of the Craven College. Special thanks are extended to members of those classes and, especially, to Tom Dugdale, who allowed me to rummage in his extensive archives, which include a pile of large scrapbooks kept by—yes, our old friend Thomas Brayshaw!

5

Kelcow Cave
A bronze FIBULA was
found here

low
ood

G

Main's Pasture

Summer Ho.

Banks

Grammar School
Free

Tott
kalds Ch.
urage
l School

Giggleswick

Hainss Head
F.S.

Bell Hill

Coal Pit

Settle Bridge

Beck House

Pump

Pump

Thames
Cottage

Sandhum
Lathe

Foot Bridge

Snuff Mill
(Cotton)

Gasometer

Mill Lane

463

454

482

Marshfield Ho.

Bondend Ho.
Quakers Meeting Ho.

Beggar's Wife Br.

Goldlands Barn

L

Gate Ho.

The Shed
(Cotton Mill)

1849

Bridge End Lathe

Weir

B.^r Stone Marked
Langcliffe & Settle divide here

Bridge End Mill
(Cotton)

M.S. LONDON 236

Ascens

Pump
Proctor's Row

SETTLE

Court Ho.

Terrace

Methodist
Primiti

Upper Se

Bollands Lane

The View from Castleberg

CASTLEBERG rises beyond the huddled buildings of Settle like a piece of operatic scenery. In the morning, it is mysterious, deep in shadow. Afternoon reveals the pearl-whiteness of its limestone. The evening sun gives it a reddish tint.

An eighteenth century engraving shows the sides of the knoll laid out with gigantic numerals, with the implication that Castleberg was used as a sun-dial. For many years, Castleberg was quarried and lumps of limestone burnt in an adjacent kiln.

In about 1800, a zig-zag route to the summit of the knoll was opened for the bravest folk. Castleberg was leased as a pleasure ground. When offered for sale in January, 1830, it was described as 'all that Romantic and Picturesque Plot, Piece or Parcel of Land & Rock...'

Anyone interested in the history of Settle and Giggleswick should begin by joining the jackdaws on Castleberg and using the famous knoll as a vantage point. Viewing the town from the heights is akin to inspecting a model townscape on an architect's table. All is revealed in fascinating detail.

Castleberg offers longer views, including part of North Ribblesdale, which is unusual among Yorkshire valleys in having a north-south orientation. Far to the left, the Ribble is seen negotiating a series of ox-bows in the spongy flatlands below the town.

Settle is an Anglian name meaning—a settlement. The Angles arrived from the west in about the seventh century. The first houses clustered beside Castleberg as though for mutual warmth. Water seeped from Castleberg into troughs on Well Hill.

School textbooks show smiling people of the medieval period operating a neat open-field village or living in hamlets surrounded by pasture and woodland.

In the craggy North-West, farmers have always done what the land and climate permit. Sixteenth century visitors to nearby Cumbria mentioned men 'who have but little tillage, by reason whereof they lyve hardly and at ease, which makyth them tall of personage and hable to endure hardness when necessyte requyryth.'

Castleberg is not the best place for studying Giggleswick, the old part of which is tucked away in a fold of the landscape beyond the River Ribble. The name Giggleswick may be Old Norse, signifying Gigel's farm or Old English—'the village with the Church'.

The Norse-Irish reached the Dales from the west, early in the tenth century. These taciturn people, who readily adapted themselves to the peripheral areas, where the landscape was knobbly and pastoral farming a necessity, were descendants of emigrants from Scandinavia who had voyaged around the top of Scotland and down to Ireland, some to marry red-haired Irish lasses. The extent of their incursion is indicated in the dale country by the use of the word 'fell' for hill.

Our view from Castleberg extends across a widening dale to a gritstone ridge marking the division between Ribblesdale and the Hodder Valley. The highspot of the ridge is Whelpstone Crag. To the right may be seen Giggleswick Common and an outcrop known as the Rocking Stone, the meeting place of five parishes.

Settle and Giggleswick lie in a favoured part of the country. The Ribble Valley opens its mouth to the mild western breezes and each winter welcomes a herd of Icelandic whooper swans to its floodwater. A half circle of hills provides Settle with bield [shelter] from the north and east.

Becks and springs yield abundant water. Good grazing for livestock is found on the grey-green hills of Craven, part of the largest outcrop of limestone in Britain. Terraces on the steeper hills near Settle are a reminder of a time when people literally scratched a living, using ox-drawn ploughs to prepare the ground for corn.

Notice the grey-blue whaleback of Pendle Hill, a bulwark of Lancashire. Until 1974, Yorkshire claimed most of Bowland and came to within 13 miles of the Irish Sea. Both Settle and Giggleswick stand in a curiously detached part of Yorkshire, lying to the west of the Pennines.

Hereabouts is the Craven Fault, an awesome fracture of the earth. Giggleswick Scar, which protects Settle from the north, is composed of almost pure limestone which, because the land cracked rather than bent, now lies cheek-by-jowl with gritstone, a much younger rock.

The road up Buckhaw Brow is on the line of the Fault. Notice how drystone walls reflect the local geology by indicating a change of rock, from grey to brown. No Pennine waller carried a stone further than he must!

The fault-line is also evident at Queen's Rock, in the bed of the Ribble. The demarcation between lime and grit occurs at the beck in Stockdale, a secluded valley above Settle, and Scaleber Foss tumbles from a lip of limestone into an area where the gritstone is well exposed, having been quarried for quernstones and building material.

Notice, as you look out from Castleberg, the smooth lines of the landscape, a tribute to the sculpturing properties of glacial ice. As what we call the Ice Age developed, fingers of ice, advancing from Lakeland into Craven, deepened and scoured the old river valleys, creating in North Ribblesdale a distinctive U-shape, and smearing its lower sides with boulder-clay.

Yet more material, deposited by the sole of the glacier, formed drumlins (cigar-shaped drift mounds), such as at Halsteads and

9

Cammock, the last name being derived from camb (Old English for the crest of a hill). The Ribble, in the days when it was unrestrained, caused extensive floods, during which alluvium (riverborne material) was deposited.

In pockets of the limestone country are deposits of blue clay, some of which was used to line the dew-ponds, saucer-like depressions which retained water for the stock in what was otherwise a free-draining area.

Giggleswick Tarn, drained as recently as 1830, had a length of half a mile and a maximum depth of twelve feet. It was noted for its fish and, when drained, yielded the remains of a 14th century dugout boat (to be seen in Leeds Museum).

The variable heights of the Ribble are evident in the shallow terraces to be seen on the valley sides. One such terrace is negotiated by anyone walking up Kirkgate at Settle.

Notice, too, as you survey the district from Castleberg, the wooded crest of Cleatop, where the Percy family, lords of Settle, had their manor house, and the lynchets (ploughing terraces) above Dog Meadow, where stood a water-powered mill.

Notice the multi-chimneyed *Falcon Hotel,* formerly Ingfield House. The 'ings' were water-meadows. Butch Lane, nearby, is named after 'butts', used in medieval times for compulsory archery practice.

The embankments, viaducts and bridges of the Settle-Carlisle neatly divide the town into two parts. A klaxon sound draws attention to a diesel train on the older railway, the 'Little' North Western, which follows a side valley towards Clapham.

During the Railway Mania of the 1840s, six schemes were outlined for bringing tracks into Settle. And before that, someone tried to raise money to build a canal.

Giggleswick School is conspicuous, with its large Victorian buildings and domed chapel. Two lines of trees heading for the

Giggleswick School Chapel

skyline indicate the course of the old coach road over High Rigg. Settle High School (which, like the Middle School, is on the Giggleswick side of the river) takes pupils from an area almost as large as the Isle of Man.

Giggleswick Scar bears a deep scar caused by quarrying. Woodland at the Mains was once coppiced, the timber being periodically clear-felled to be made into bobbins. Smearsett, overlooking the upper dale, is named 'sett' after *saeter,* the summer grazing ground of Norse folk.

From Castleberg, Old Settle is revealed as a picturesque huddle of 17th and 18th century buildings; they seem to jostle each other around the market place and along some of the principal streets.

Years ago, Cheapside and Kirkgate heard the tinkle of the bell on the leading horse of a packhorse train or a coach fresh from the heights of Hunter Bark where, before the Turnpike was made, the old road north had its most exciting stretch.

Lost among the buildings are a few remaining examples of Settle yards and ginnels, including the narrow thoroughfare off Cheapside which generations of children called 'Spooky Alley'. The yards, created by infilling, were invariably known after their owners—Bowskill's Yard, Howson's Yard, Tatham's Yard, Radcliffe's Yard, and others...

Elsewhere are less pretty patterns of Victorian terraces and Council house estates, including Northfield, from which as recently as the 1939-45 war—when the North Field was still open land—crops of potatoes were lifted.

Look for the gleaming facade of *Ye Olde Naked Man* cafe, formerly an inn, the name being a skit at the over-elaborate clothing fashions favoured by the well-to-do of the seventeenth century.

The Town Hall, built in the 1830s in pseudo-Jacobean style, shows off rows of tall chimneys. It stands on the site of the Tollbooth, where the Watchman had his quarters, the Big Jury met to ponder on local affairs and the town's measures were kept.

Almost at the base of Castleberg is the yard of the *Talbot,* formerly the Dog Inn, named after a rare breed kept by the Talbots of Bashall Hall, Bowland. When Settle had several tanpits, the *Talbot* was the favourite meeting place of leather-dealers.

Incline your head to the right for a view of the capacious roof of the Co-op and, beyond, the broad spread of roof-slates marking Holy Ascension, a daughter church of Giggleswick. The bells are no longer rung, the impressive sound of bells emanating from a recording. The graveyard at Settle, now fully occupied, is so hemmed in and wet in places it was said that being buried here was the next best thing to burial at sea.

Beyond the railway lies the green oblong of the cricket field, part of the Langcliffe Hall Estate. A big-hitter of years ago drove a cricket ball 72 miles. (It fell into the compartment of a train and

and was found at Carlisle).

Industry is represented by the ponderous architecture of King's Mill by the river and the gargantuan Creamery, situated on an industrial estate with the venerable but unlovely name of Sowarth.

The local reach of the river was fordable at a place still known as Kendalman's, after the Westmorland pack-horse men. Another major ford lay near Gildersleets. In those days, the Ribble, unrestrained by walls and buildings, was broad and shallow enough in places for a ford to become established. (There is a place in the slow-running Tems Beck at Giggleswick where sand habitually gathers to such an extent it was collected by a local builder).

Trees on the side of Giggleswick Scar hide the remains of half a dozen lime kilns which were in use almost 200 years ago. Also in the wood are traces of the retaining wall built when pieces of displaced limestone began to fall on to the Turnpike road and became a menace to traffic.

Old Giggleswick is not visible from Castleberg. The church which once presided over a parish covering about 30 square miles, is out of sight. On the present parish boundary is Dead Man's Cave! The village occupies a snug position between High Rigg and Huntworth.

Barns and outbuildings now adapted for housing were used for their traditional purposes within living memory. Jack Brassington tells of the regular progress of cattle through the village from their shippon at the bottom of Belle Hill to Tems Beck where they drank.

Names on the map evoke the old days. West of Settle is Coney Garth, where rabbits were bred for their flesh and pelts. Further west, at Cockett Moss, lay deposits of peat, used in the domestic grate. Good peat warmed a man twice—once when he had cut it and once when he sat beside a fire formed of the aromatic turves.

Castleberg itself, when viewed from Settle Market Place, has a grandeur which has appealed to visitors since, in the Romantic Period (1760-1820), gentlefolk with taste and leisure visited the limestone country as part of an excursion to the Lake District.

Castleberg was feared by the old-time Settlers because it jettisoned rocks. Mr Moffatt, the parson of Zion Chapel, fearing that stones from a frost-weakened outcrop would break loose, roll down the hill and damage the building, inquired about insurance cover.

He was told: 'If anything like that happened, sir, we'd regard it as an Act of God.' Mr Moffatt quietly pointed out that the God he worshipped would never do such a thing as drop stones on the chapel.

From the Domesday book.

14

Lords and
Overlords

Norman William.

THE Domesday Book, compiled by Norman scribes, had the mundane object of providing a statistical survey of English society as it was in 1086 AD. By the time of this great survey, the population of the Yorkshire Dales was probably no more than 3,000.

The Norman Conquest petered out at the northern fells of the Bowland district, beyond which was a buffer zone, with lands somewhat loosely held by David, the Scottish King; hence the omission from Domesday of most of Cumberland and Westmorland.

Land between the Ribble and the Mersey, which was to become part of Lancashire, was included in a section headed *Terra inter Ripam et Mersham* (occupying only two pages of the survey) while to the north of the Ribble lay Yorkshire, extending from sea to sea.

After dealing with the Yorkshire Ridings (the word *riding* being Old Norse, meaning one-third), the compilers of the Domesday Book added a section which they headed 'In Craven'. This included Settle and Giggleswick, tiny settlements in a poor, remote,

15

border district which was flanked by high and barren moorland. No one was quite sure where the boundary lay.

The North Country, including our own district, still bore evidence of the Harrying of the North, more precisely Yorkshire— a campaign of genocide, burning and looting which, in the period 1069-71, was Norman William's response to rebellion.

The death toll has been estimated to total about 100,000 people. Over vast areas, wrote a chronicler, referring to an area to the east, 'nothing moves among the ruins of the burnt-out villages but packs of wolves and wild dogs tearing at the bodies of the dead.'

Not until 1092 was Cumbria taken from the Scots by William Rufus, who led an army through to Carlisle. Six years earlier, when the Domesday commissioners went on their rounds, information was sparse and many a Yorkshire manor was recorded as 'waste', a legacy of Norman vengeance.

Roger of Poitou, son of Roger de Montgomery, a principal adviser to the Conqueror, had been granted the new Honour of Lancaster [which embraced Giggleswick, presumably because it lay west of the Pennines]. The lord's name appears in the Domesday survey, which related to land use and the taxable value of each holding.

Our story of Settle and Giggleswick begins with Domesday and the realisation that when the Normans arrived they found a well-organised and prospering society in which Anglian, Norse and Celtic folk had a part.

All the villages with which we are familiar were then established and, despite the unfamiliar spellings, they are readily identifiable: Ghigeleswick (Giggleswick), Rodemele (Rathmell), Prestune (Long Preston), Stainforde (Stainforth), Wiclesforde (Wigglesworth), Setel (Settle), Lanclif (Langcliffe) and Stacuse (Stackhouse).

We are also made aware of important landowners, with short, sharp names—Fech, Ulf, Bu, Feg and Carle. We are informed about the extent of their holdings. The land measurements include a bovate or oxgang and a carucate. The bovate represented from eight to 15 acres, depending on the type of land concerned, and a carucate was assessed at roughly eight bovates or, classically, the area an ox-team was capable of ploughing in a year.

Fech, of Giggleswick, had four carucates for tax (property of equivalent value to a carucate of land). Bu had three carucates of land for tax at Anley and three carucates in Settle. At Anley, under the heading of Land of the King (presumably claimed by the Conqueror following Earl Edwin's rebellion) was the soke mill, where local people had to take their corn to be ground.

My lord received no money for this service; the 'soke' was the retention of a proportion of the meal. Historians now refer to Yorkshire 'sokes', a group of settlements, bound by overlordship and its attendant dues and services to the seat of the overlord. In such a 'multiple estate', both upland and lowland communities might be bound together.

The mill at Anley (on a site now occupied by Runley Farm) had a waterwheel turned not by the Ribble but a tributary beck flowing from the hills at Springfield, crossing Watery Lane and (nowadays) passing under the Settle-Carlisle Railway before blending its water with the main river.

Old Anley is now represented by a a group of farm buildings in a field near Cleatop. The Domesday Book made no mention of a church at Giggleswick, which suggests that the early building was ruined.

Roger of Poitou, fickle in his loyalties, ultimately lost all (1102), but not before he had granted Bowland—and probably also Giggleswick—to Robert de Lacy, whose family built a castle on a limestone knoll at Clitheroe (1100).

The manors of the far-flung Giggleswick parish subsequently became part of the great Percy Fee and thus, despite their location to the west of the Pennine watershed, were firmly in Yorkshire, as they have remained to this day.

The Percy family sprang into prominence with William de Percy. He was in attendance on the Conqueror on his return to England in 1067. Henry de Percy, who was granted 100 manors in Yorkshire, had a restless nature which impelled him to become a Crusader. He died within sight of Jerusalem (1097).

The Percies were associated with the Settle district for over four centuries until 1537. Their manor house was Cleatop and their estate extended to Merebeck [boundary stream] and to where the old road crossed the moor between Settle and Long Preston. They bought Allestedes [Halsteads] and Cambok [Cammock].

Under the Percies the 'soke' system, which was never popular with the tenants, did at least give stability to local life. The tenantry paid their dues to the overlord at his court and made themselves available, when necessary in times of emergency, to form what was in effect a private army to defend the King's interests.

Much of the northern hill country might be classified as forest [preserved for hunting]. Some was Royal forest, available for the King's pleasure. The majority were the playground of the big landowners, who pursued the red deer and wild boar.

Richard de Percy, a 'bold spirited man' [which means he was wild and lawless] distinguished himself as one of the leaders of the Barons at the time of Magna Carta. Henry de Percy (1228-1272), of Cleatop, the son of William, married Eleanor Plantagent, a niece of the king.

He is especially well remembered as the man who obtained from Henry III the right to hold a fair and market in Settle and to receive the tolls. This first market charter, granted in 1249, was the start of the Tuesday market, which is held to this day.

My lord was also granted the right to hold a fair 'on the eve, day and morrow of the feast of St Laurence each year for ever with all the liberties and free customs usually appertaining unless such fair be to the detriment of neighbouring markets or fairs.'

Settle was now on course for great development. Giggleswick was to remain what it is today—a relatively quiet village.

Monastic Influence

FOR some four hundred years, the development of our area was largely in the hands of the monks, especially the Cistercians who became established at Fountains, Furness and Salley [the old name for Sawley].

Their North Ribblesdale and Malham estates were built up by generous grants of land, much of it marginal land and upland which was ripe for development.

The Cistercians were White Monks, so called because they wore long robes made of undyed wool. Their order was founded in Burgundy with the object, in decadent times, of permitting a return to the austerity and strict conduct of the first Benedictines. In some cases, Cistercian communities were established in this country by Benedictine dissidents.

In their spread from France, the Cistercians found in Yorkshire a largely empty landscape, much of it still 'waste' from the Harrying. Norman lords, inheritors of vast tracts of country, were stern but devout.

Their grants of lands to the monks were, in most cases, of the less productive areas. Alfred of Rievaulx, an early Cistercian abbey in Yorkshire, hinted at the conditions when he wrote: 'Our food is scanty, our garments rough, our drink is from the stream and our sleep often upon our book. Under our tired limbs there is but hard mat; when sleep is sweetest, we must rise at the bell's bidding. . .'

19

Through their gifts to the abbeys, the Norman lords were ensuring the goodwill of the Church on earth and the intercessions of the holy men in the Hereafter.

For their part, the Cistercians managed to serve God and Mammon. They came from a part of France where people were skilled at making iron and at pastoral farming, especially the rearing of sheep.

The high land of Craven soon became an extensive sheep range. The constant nibbling of the sheep rid the area of the coarser vegetation and prevented the natural regeneration of trees. Big open pastures were created.

The employees of the monks milked the ewes and locked up the goodness of the milk as cheese. They sold the fleeces, many to foreign dealers. In short, the descendants of men who came to Yorkshire dedicated to the simple, austere life were soon presiding over vast estates. About half of the parish of Giggleswick became monastic land.

Gifts and grants continued to arrive at the abbeys, some from small-time landowners who had the medieval fear of being roasted over the fires of Hell. The title deeds were a form of insurance policy, ensuring an easy passage to Heaven. Cistercians offered immunity from ex-communication by any Bishop to those who showed generosity towards them.

Monastic enterprise was reflected in the passage of officials between the abbeys and outlying granges, or farms, some tracks linking together to permit Fountains to keep in touch with estates as far away as Borrowdale, at the heart of the Lake District. Furness Abbey also had great possessions in that area.

In the old parish of Giggleswick, the principal monastic landowners were Fountains, Furness and Sawley. Jervaulx (Wensleydale) had a large estate in North Ribblesdale.

William de Percy, of Cleatop (1112-1168) gave the Moors and

Tarn of Malham to Fountains Abbey, which had been established (1132) by a party of monks from York. William founded Sawley Abbey in the valley of the Ribble.

About the year 1160, Adam, son of Meldred de Giggleswick, 'grants to God and St Mary and the monks of Furness a carucate of land called Stacus [Stackhouse].' With it, for a rent of 10s a year, went rights in Giggleswick Wood concerning the feeding of swine and cutting of timber for building purposes. The monks were also permitted to use the common pastures of Giggleswick and Stackhouse.

Craven was mainly sheep country. Sheep from Fountains Fell were driven to the grange at Kilnsey to be washed, then clipped. The fleeces were borne in ox-hauled wains across the moorland roads to Fountains Abbey. The granges of Newby and Colt Park consigned wool to Furness Abbey, which stood close to the gleaming sands of Morecambe Bay.

The Craven climate, being frequently cloudy and wet, was unsuited to the growing of corn. Perhaps one in three crops was successful. When Sawley was founded, the dismal conditions (*in terra nebulosa et pluviosa*) did not allow the ears of corn to ripen; they rotted on the stalk. An appeal for help to the Pope led to the abbey being given the living of Gargrave.

Sawley land met Fountains land at the head of Silverdale, above Stainforth. The marker was Ulfkil Cross [the base of which was only recently moved from the roadside to an adjacent field]. Sawley produced scholars as well as saints. Among those trained here was William de Rymington, who became Chancellor of Oxford and afterwards returned to his own abbey as Prior.

In the 13th century, the Pudsay family, having acquired the patronage of Giggleswick Church, presented the income of the parish to the Benedictines of Finchdale Abbey, in Durham. The Prior and Convent of Finchdale were placed in charge of the parish, by a Bull of Pope Gregory IX, on March 11, 1232. The monks were content to farm out the tithes and let out the property.

Finchale Priory, after the Dissolution.

The Furness monks, having grants at Stackhouse, violated the rights of Elias de Giggleswick, the local lord, by building a corn mill. The monks, being merely tenants, was out of order in challenging Elias's monopoly for grinding corn.

The situation was complicated by the fickle nature of the Ribble which, between Stackhouse [in the township of Giggleswick] and Langcliffe, split into several channels, flowing between islands composed of alluvium. The monks had built their mill on Stackhouse Holme, which belonged to Langcliffe. The lord of Langcliffe was—Elias.

Furness brought the matter to the attention of the Pope's legate, who in 1221 decreed that Elias should take possession of the mill and be allowed to rent the mill-pond. The monks improved their position by being granted a trifling sum annually as an acknowledgement and being released from their obligation to pay rent.

The Abbot of Furness thus became lord of Stackhouse, though subsequently Furness showed very little interest in the property. This abbey did own other land in the dale, this being a tract which took in the southern slopes of Ingleborough and extended across to Ling Gill.

Elias gave his mill and lands at Langcliffe and Rathmell to the abbey at Sawley. When, about 1255, he was old and weary, he resigned his manor of Giggleswick to Henry de Percy and received in return a pension of 24 marks, paid to him at Sawley Abbey. Then, like so many others, he arranged that both he and his wife would in due course be buried there.

Robert of Settle granted Sawley some land 'with my body for burial there.' The monks received Stockdale from Richard de Morville. The precise details were 'all uthulnesmire [Attermire] and thence Wifvesdalall [possibly Wise Haw, a pasture near Capon Hall] and as far as the land of Settle reaches from the top of the said At'mir Langclif to the boundaries of Airton [the watershed between Ribble and Aire].'

After a lusty growth, and a period of consolidation, the North Country abbeys went into a steady line, becoming too worldy and suffering from Scottish raids and the insidious Black Death. The Abbots found it increasingly difficult to pay back debts which accrued from ambitious building schemes.

Meanwhile, the farming descendants of Anglian settlers continued their patient work, clearing trees in a landscape which was still largely open, there being few walls to divide up the properties. Heavy ploughs were used on the better ground, and terraces created on the hillside for arable crops are evidence of the need to take every opportunity to produce food.

Limestone was incinerated in rough kilns, using timber as fuel, the whole being sodded over for controlled burning. The lime had uses on buildings and sweetened sour land.

Raiders from Scotland

THE abbeys provided easy pickings for raiders who, crossing the Anglo-Scottish border, penetrated deeply into England by way of the north-south valley of the Eden.

A raid of 1138 was little more than a sortie by an armed band. Two centuries later, after the English reverses at Bannockburn, the incursions were intense.

It was a depressing time. 'Never yet was there such misery in the land,' wrote a chronicler. 'Christ slept and all his saints.' War and pestilence, crop failure and diseases of farmstock, combined to form a catalogue of despair.

Craven was still mourning the death of Henry de Percy (1315). The young and fit members of the community were exhausted by long spells of military duty on the border.

Scottish raids were recorded in 1316 and 1318. During late November, 1319, the Scotch rebels 'burnt the towns of Spofford...Gisburne in Craven, Setel, Gigleswick...Stanford, Langclif, and Rowthemell.' The Scots penetrated as far south as Castleford, calling at Settle again during their return journey.

Daily Life

WHEN the Scots had departed, Giggleswick re-grouped itself about the Church. Settle continued to huddle close to Castleberg or by the road which came down from the moor and along Kirkgate. The new Langcliffe is thought to have been sited half a mile to the south of where the old village had stood.

In those self-reliant days, a family with spinning wheel and simple loom made its own clothing. Leather outer garments were ideal for cheating the bad weather. Flax was available (for making linen) and hemp (for cords and ropes). The drying grounds for fabric and hides are recalled at Giggleswick by field names—Tenters and The

Fellins respectively.

The growing season was too late and cold for wheat and the most suitable crop was oats, which—as already related—did not always ripen satisfactorily. The several manorial mills in Giggleswick parish had kilns attached for roasting oats before they were ground. Oatmeal, served as porridge or oatcake, was a staple food.

In winter, when meat was of the salted variety, the dreams of the peasantry must have been coloured by thoughts of fresh red meat, such as that being consumed by the well-to-do, who had their deer parks, pigeon cotes and fishponds. Anyone who killed a free-ranging red deer hit the culinary jackpot.

The residents of Giggleswick who paid the poll tax in 1379 included Wilhelmus Monk, Willelmus de Laukland, Walterus Forstre, Nicholaus Skynner, Laurencius de Armetsted and Adam de Palay. In addition, to subsidise King Richard II in the war against France, a tax was levied on everyone over 16 years old.

The precise sum was based on a person's state and degree— fourpence for an ordinary householder, sixpence for a tradesman and twelvepence for the better-end. Richard de Bank of Giggleswick, who paid twelvepence, was probably a merchant or an innkeeper.

Of a total of £604.19s.4d raised in the West Riding, the 52 taxpayers of Setle [Settle] found 17s.10d and 53 people in Gygleswyk [Giggleswick] paid £1.1.8d. Compare these figures with those of £3.0.4d for Leeds and £1.3s for Bradford.

York versus Lancaster

THE Wars of the Roses were part of a family squabble [between York and Lancaster] which took place at a time when London was remote, having little influence on northern politics.

Giggleswick parish was staunchly Lancastrian. The Percy family, the overlords, retained their allegiance to the Crown, partly because they were feuding with the Nevilles, who had close marriage ties with the House of York.

The district suffered for its adherence to Lancaster. Edward IV wreaked vengeance, even against churches. Giggleswick Church was virtually re-built when tolerance returned to the national life.

Worshippers had a lasting reminder of the Wars in the effigy of Sir Richard Tempest, former Lord of Knight Stainforth, which stood close to the spot where he was buried along with the head of his charger.

Sir Richard, born about 1425, was knighted at the Battle of Wakefield in 1460 but was attainted for treason in the following year. He was pardoned by Edward IV and died in 1488. Also buried in church were two wives—Dame Sibill and Dame Mabel.

The Pudsay family, who owned property in Settle, had their main residence at Bolton-by-Bowland, where they sheltered the fugitive king, Henry VI, after the Battle of Hexham.

Men at Arms

AN integral part of the feudal system was the requirement that every fit man should muster when required for service under his lord. Each person had to provide himself with weapons according to his means.

This happened when Henry, Lord Clifford, led a Craven contingent to Flodden Field for the decisive battle against the Scots [September 9, 1513]. Using the muster roll, Nicholson, a Victorian poet, wrote:

> Old Giggleswick, beneath her scraggy scar,
> Had fifty sons, who bravely fought in war.

Among the names on the list was Robt. Stakhouse, who possessed a bow, horse and harness and ille also; and John Brashay, 'a bowe.' The Bowmen of Settyll [Settle] included Rich. Browne, Will-m Talyr, Rogr. Yveson, Hug. Carr and Gyles Kokeson.

A Chantry School

GIGGLESWICK Church had two family chantries, associated with the Stainfords and Tempests respectively. A third chantry was founded by a priest named James Carr who in an indenture of 1499 is described as a chantry priest required to 'pray for the sowle of the Founder and all Xpen sowles' and to sing certain Masses.

James Carr shared his knowledge with the parishioners and his flair for teaching attracted several pupils. He was moved to found a gramer scole [grammar school] for local boys.

On November 12, 1507, a lease was entered into between 'the right reverend ffader in Gode, Thomas, Prior of Deresme [Durham] and Convent of the same on the one partie, by James Karr, prieste, on the other partie'.

James was given a 79 year lease of half one acre of land with the 'appertenance laitlye in the haldying of Richard Lemyng [Leeming] near the church garth of Gyllswyke in Craven within the countie of York'.

When James died (1518), the teaching was continued by nominees of the Vicar and Churchwardens. It was the beginning of a school which (after the dissolution of the Chantries) became Giggleswick Grammar School, receiving a Royal Charter from Edward VI in 1553. At this time, the School had eight Governors, a Headmaster and an Usher.

In 1592, the Governors exhibited to the Archbishop of York certain 'wholesome statutes and ordinances' whereby the School was to be governed. One requirement was that 'the Scholemaster shall not use in Schoole any language to his schollers which be of ryper yeares and proceadinges but only the Lattyne, Greeke and Hebrewe, nor shall willingly permit the use of the Englishe tonge in the Schoole to them which are or shal be able to speake lattyne'.

Any scholar who did not meet this requirement was 'returned to his frendes to be broughte upp in some other honest trade and exercyse of lyfe.'

The Master of Giggleswick was to teach impartially 'the Poor as well as the Rich, and the Parishioner as well as the Stranger.'

Dissolution of the Monasteries

THE end of the medieval period was marked by the Dissolution of the great monastic estates, which passed to the Crown. In the north, it was a profound shock for many, who supported an uprising which became known as the Pilgrimage of Grace.

Sir Richard Tempest of Bracewell wrote to Thomas Cromwell, who had been promoted Visitor-General of the Monasteries, reporting that unrest occurred in the summer of 1535 at the mere hint of the closure of an Abbey and that over 300 people, having rioted in Craven, 'have cast down houses, dykes and hedges about Gykylswyke'.

In the following year, an Act was passed dissolving any abbey with an income of less than £200 a year. Among such abbeys was Sawley, the monks being turned out in May. Six months later, an armed rebellion by tenants and labourers on abbey lands caused consternation.

It began in Lincolnshire and spread to York. The first Dales stirrings in what was essentially a northern rising were detected around Dent, Sedbergh and Wensleydale.

The Pilgrims were demonstrating in the belief that Thomas Cromwell was out to destroy religious life, but (as usual) they were joined by some who had economic grievances and saw an opportunity of expressing them in defiance of the law. The Percy family offered no backing; they did not want to be associated with such lowly folk. Abbots and monks, taken by surprise, did their best to avoid being incriminated.

The leaders of the rebels, now desperate men, ordered that lords and gentry should be taken and invited to take an oath of allegiance. The alternative would be death.

Sir Stephen Hammerton, of Wigglesworth Hall, arrested in 1537 for siding with the rebellion, claimed that the first he knew of the insurrection was when he heard that a proclamation concerning a parish meeting had been posted on the door of Giggleswick Church.

Arriving at Giggleswick, he found the notice had been removed and borne off to the meeting, which he understood to be 'above Neales yng', possibly at Ulfkil Cross. Sir Stephen was surrounded by about 300 armed men and forced to take the oath.

The Pilgrimage of Grace fizzled out. Among those put to death was the Abbot of Sawley. At its dissolution in 1539, Fountains owned 2,336 horned cattle, 1,326 sheep, 86 horses and 79 swine.

The Crown now held the monastic estates, but not for long. Costly wars on the Continent led to a rocketing inflation and such a need for money that the estates had to be sold off, fragmented, some pieces of land going to local landowners anxious to increase their holdings and others to speculators.

With the establishment of the Church of England, those who kept to the Old Faith and refused to attend services of the Established Church were known as recusants [Latin-*recusare*].

Giggleswick, being close to Lancashire, had several families who retained a strong love of Catholicism. The recusants sometimes evaded capture by the Justices by crossing the county border. Justices had jurisdiction only in their own county.

Among the Giggleswick recusants were Hugh Clapham and Elena, his wife, who had been married secretly, at night, in a house near Waddington, with a Catholic priest in attendance.

Richard Frankland, of Giggleswick, was accused in 1596 of having his child secretly baptised as a Catholic. The baptism may have occurred at Lawkland Hall, the home of John and Ann Ingleby. They partly re-built their home in 1586, at which time a 'secret room', to be used in emergency as a hiding place for the priest, was probably built.

Despite his professed love of learning, Henry VIII did much harm to the rudimentary education system and the number of schools declined.

Giggleswick grammar school not only survived; in 1553 the first endowment from an outside source was received. Edward VI ordained there should be a grammar school in the village—despite the fact that one had been in existence for half a century!

In 1599, Christopher Shute, vicar of Giggleswick, with other governors, made the School prosper as never before. Among the benefactions was the gift of a sum of money 'towards a potacioun [potation] amongst the poore schollers...on Sainte Gregorie's daie [March 12].'

Laws and 'Paines'

AT Settle and Giggleswick, the Percy family were succeeded as lords by the Clifford family, of Skipton. They were major landowners in Craven and also in the upper Eden Valley.

In the redistribution of monastic property, the estates of Sawley Abbey came into the hands of Sir Arthur Darcy, a land speculator.

At Settle, resentment built up over the soke mill at Runley Bridge, now owned by speculators, who were making an exorbitant profit. The law being un-reformed, legal battles over the mill were costly—and pointless.

Giggleswick's 'boke [book] of the order of the Court nominating the Lawes & by lawes within the Townshippe' governed local behaviour and the severity of the paine [penalty] to be imposed on those who broke one of those laws.

No stranger was permitted to take bracken from Slaidbanke. The out-Dykes [drystone walls] around the fields at 'Giglesweeke' must be 'a yard & a half high'. It was prohibited to lay hemp in a watercourse above 'Giglesweeke towne'.

No one was allowed to pill [peel] bark from oak, ash, holly or elder within the Lordship of Giggleswick. Alehouse keepers were not allowed to serve drink or food during the time of Divine Service.

There must be no wool-gathering in the fields 'before the Cattle be all gone forth'. No wool should be gathered on the Scar before Midsummer. A fuller was not allowed to dress any cloth in the water running through Giggleswick between 6 a.m. and 9 p.m. Each township had an obligation to maintain archery butts, those at Giggleswick being situated on land behind the Church.

Ebbing and Flowing Well

THE seepage of water from Giggleswick Scar and Huntworth Common provided the village with copious fresh water. A roadside well became renowned through what was written about it. Strangers marvelled, when looking into a stone trough, that the water 'ebbed and flowed'. [One theory is that a double syphon exists in the rock behind the well].

In 1598, a poet named Michael Drayton toured Britain, composing lines about the principal points of interest. The first part of his project, spread over 18 books, was entitled Polyolbion (1613). Drayton, fascinated by the Ebbing and Flowing Well at the foot of Giggleswick Scar, wrote:

At Giggleswick, where I a fountain can you show,
That eight times in a day is said to ebb and flow.

Drayton was not content with speculation about natural curiosities. He brought along some nymphs. Rather more down-to-earth was the composition of Richard Braithwaite, of Kendal, in 1638:

Neither know the learnd'st that travell
What procures it, salt or gravel.

Civil War

THE heady rush into a new age, following the Dissolution of the Monasteries and the liberalisation of trade, was delayed by the Civil War.

Henry Clifford, the fifth and last Earl of Cumberland, was a Royalist. His lead was followed by other gentry in Craven. It was ironical that another son of Craven, John Lambert, born at Calton above Malhamdale, became a distinguished Parliamentary general.

The Clifford castle at Skipton was besieged for three years, although clearly the beseigers were less than vigilant. Royalists slipped through their lines to replenish their supplies.

The folk of Giggleswick and Settle would see a constant coming and going of armed parties, two of which, according to tradition, had a skirmish at Gildersleets, an incident which may be borne out by an entry in the parish register of Skipton for December 23, 1642—that Edward Waddington was 'slayne at Settle'.

Signature of Henry, Earl of Cumberland, on a Giggleswick Church charter

Richard Horsfall, of Neils Ing, served as captain of a troop of Royalist horse and, surrendering to the Parliament, took no further part in the war.

In December, 1643, John Lambert, stayed at Giggleswick, possibly at Beck Hall [now Beck House]. With Parliamentary contempt for the Established Church, he arranged for his troops to be billeted in the building.

In 1644, when the Parliamentary forces were supreme in Yorkshire and King Charles found sanctuary in Scotland, the first phase of the Civil War came to an end. The opening shots of the second phase were heard in 1648 when, with the King now a prisoner of Cromwell, friends in Scotland attempted to rescue him.

An army was mustered by the Duke of Hamilton. In the vanguard were English Royalists under Sir Marmaduke Langdale. The army marched up Edenvale and took Appleby Castle before advancing on Preston. On their left flank was John Lambert and his forces. Cromwell and his men advanced from the south. The Parliamentary forces joined up at Otley in August.

Hamilton's main force passed through Lancaster and Hornby. It would have been a spectacular sight when Langdale, with 3,000 foot and 800 horse, occupied Settle as part of a plan to move in on Skipton Castle and wrest it from its Parliamentary garrison.

The soldiers 'made havoc of the country'. [Lieut Arthur Catteral, of Giggleswick, when claiming compensation from the King at the Restoration, valued at £29 the goods 'taken by Captayne Ripon's souldgers.']

The Parliamentary army travelled westwards from Skipton and battle took place near Preston, after which Cromwell returned to Skipton, where he penned his despatch.

In 1651, King Charles II made a dramatic journey from Scotland to Worcester, his force using the Edenvale route and travelling so quickly that Cromwell's men were left behind in Scotland.

John Lambert, with a force of cavalry, set off in pursuit. He was at Settle on August 11, and in a despatch he wrote to the Council of State in London, he mentioned 'we are this night with five of our best regiments of horse quartered at Settle in Craven...The enemy as we hear are quartered about Lancaster. They have not above 4,000 horse and dragoons, and 8,000 foot, and these are very sickly and drop off daily.'

Cromwell, following Lambert, joined up and surrounded the Royalists at Worcester. Thus ended the Civil War.

The grief remained. Lieut Catteral, of Giggleswick, was left to ponder on his experiences. During the conflict, he had been injured, captured and robbed of his goods.

Meanwhile, 'my wife and six smale children could naither keep horse nor cow nor close fit to weare upon Sunday but by conveying them to nightbour houses...And when Oliver [Cromwell] set forth his Act of grace as there wasunt much in it I came home and one Mr Johnsons Justice of the peace sent for me and tould me I was a dangerus person against the Common weale and without good bondsmen he would commit me and soa I stud bound from one Session to another that it cost me six pownds...'

Constable and Overseer

AT the Restoration, confidence was restored and trade boomed, though Giggleswick and Settle were still linked to the world by rough tracks. Along them came pack-horses, some bearing corn purchased in lowland areas.

Rising from the ashes of feudalism was a yeoman class, consisting of people who owned their own freehold, perhaps purchasing it from those speculators who had bought the confiscated property of the abbeys.

Some of the Giggleswick surnames are familiar: Armitstead,

Carr, Foster, Paley, Lawson, Preston, Bankes, Clapham, Stackhouse and Brayshaw.

Justices of the Peace, appointed by the Crown, maintained the law of the land. Locally, Bylawmen or Bylawgreaves (voted in by local people) and Constables, (appointed at Easter, the duties falling on each householder in rotation) were appointed.

The system was financed by sessments (assessments, the equivalent of rates) and gaulds (rates levied for some special expense). Violation of a by-law led to the imposition of a paine (penalty).

By-laws at Giggleswick in 1602 mention a field yat (entrance to the common fields) and the edish (second flush of grass in the meadows). The farmstock included horses, cattle, sheep and 'flockes of geese'.

Giggleswick Scars were stinted for sheep grazing, a 'stint' representing the pasturage of a sheep and the number of animals being regulated for the good of the herbage.

Wells and watercourses must be kept pure. No one was allowed to 'lye any ffish or fflesh or any other Hurtfull thing to steepe it St Awkeld well in pane of every time iiiid.'

Everyone who rode 'of the Northfield, being the Church footway between Settle and Giggleswick Bridge' had to pay 3s.4d. A similar sum was imposed on the owner of straying swine. Anyone who 'shall drive ye bulle from the towne pasture called Scaleber' between certain dates must pay 6d to the Lord and a similar sum to the bylawmen.

The Constable tracked down criminals and took them for trial. He had authority to distrain on the goods of any who failed to pay their rates, tithes or taxes.

Each township had an Overseer, one of whose jobs was to distribute part of the poor rate to local paupers. He also arranged for premiums to be paid when the children of paupers were taking up apprenticeships.

The Overseer arranged for lodgings and food for any passing tramps in the Workhouse. In the late 17th century, this was not an onerous task.

The Divines

RELIGION had become stuffy. Evangelists were at hand to open the windows and admit a draught of cold, clear air. The first efforts were not appreciated.

In about 1653, William Dewsbury, who had been much moved by the witness of George Fox, the founder of Quakerism, arrived at Settle on market day, stood beside the cross and 'proclaimed the terrible day of the Lord, which was hastening and coming upon the ungodly and workers of iniquity.'

Dewsbury's reward was to be dragged from the cross, beaten and abused. The battered preacher was given aid and hospitality at the home of John and Alice Armistead. This house became a meeting place for the first local Quakers.

John Camm, attempting to preach at Settle on Market Day, was roughly handled and rescued by John Kidd of Upper Settle, 'where there was a meeting in the evening, and then things relating to the kingdom of God were plainly laid down by him.'

Quakerism's most distinguished adherent, Samuel Watson of Knight Stainforth, had made a name for himself as one who actively challenged the monopoly of Settle soke mill. He paid for this with a term in York gaol, where he had his faith strengthened through encounters with Quakers. He joined them in refusing to pay tithes.

In December, 1659, Samuel interrupted a service in Giggleswick Church [attendance at which was compulsory]. He 'spake among ye people as he was moved of God. But after a litle some of ye

St. Alkleda's Church, Giggleswick

rudest sort pulled him down and brok his head upon ye seates and having haled him out threw him downe upon ye ice.'

One Quaker, who was said to be 'revelation mad', was moved of the spirit to go to church 'to reprehend the congregation.' He did so while stark naked, carrying a burning candle.

George Fox, en route for imprisonment in Lancaster Castle, stayed overnight at Giggleswick in 1665. Weakened by imprisonment and the rigours of the journey, he had little sleep for his captors 'sat drinking all the night in the room by me. . .Next day we came to a market-town, where several Friends came to see me. . .'

When the Toleration Act of 1689 was passed, among the first of the 'Quaker places' to be licensed was 'the house of Samuel Watson at Stainforth in Giggleswick.'

One of many Anglican clergyment ejected from their livings for refusing to obey the Act of Uniformity and use the prescribed Book of Common Prayer, was Richard Frankland (1630-1698).

He returned to his native Rathmell with a wife and two children and, in 1670, defied the law by starting an Academy for the training of Nonconformist minsters. Frankland did this despite much opposition from the clergy of Craven. His type of college was exempted from the Toleration Act.

This gentle man was well disposed towards the Church of England, in which he had been reared and ordained. All his seven children had Church baptisms and in 1677 he paid rent for no less than three pews in Giggleswick Church. Yet he was excommunicated in Giggleswick Church—twice [1680 and 1690].

Shortly before his death, in October, 1698, he took part in an ordination at Rathmell when nine of his pupils were set apart for the ministry. At that time, Frankland's Academy had 50 pupils. He was buried at Giggleswick on October 5.

Building in Stone

A WELL-TO-DO family proclaimed its status, and its faith in the future, by building a house of the native stone. A datestone, complete with initials, was placed above the main door.

The Settle district is rich in seventeenth century venacular architecture and datestones. In some respects, the second half of the 17th century was the 'golden age' of the town, and it shows in the money spent on new property.

Settle straddled an 'arterial' road between the two great cities of York and Lancaster and betwixt the woollen markets of Keighley and Kendal. Pack-horse traffic was a regular sight, the sturdy animals bearing loads of wool, leather, broadcloth and knitted goods.

What was more natural, in affluent times, than to pull down the old penthouse dwellings [commented on by early tourists] and to re-built in stone, incorporating the latest ideas. Giggleswick examples of the attractive yet unpretentious dwellings of the later part of the 17th century are Ivy Fold (1669) and Sutcliffe House (built by Hugh Stackhouse, 1693).

At Settle, the splendid Folly (1675) was created for Richard Preston, a tanner and possibly the man who, about 1650, with three others, leased the parish corn mills and annoyed the locals by raising the charge for grinding corn.

Settle abounded in alehouses and had far more inns than was warranted by the size of the local population. The *Golden Lion* was first mentioned in 1654. The inn now renowned as the *Naked Man* (1663) bears the initials JC [probably John Cookson].

The Old Routes

THE old north-south route, from Long Preston to Settle, 'above Cleatop', was a high road in a literal sense, clearing the 1,000 ft contour near Hunter Bark. A continuation of the road from Giggleswick lay over High Rigg to Lawkland.

The principal means of transporting goods or bringing in supplies was the pack-horse train of 20 or more animals moving in 'line ahead' along narrow ways and across simple, one-arched bridges. The pack-horse system was evolving in monastic times and found no equal until the roads were improved in the Turnpike age.

The stocky horses, which might be of the Fell breed, which was predominantly dark, or the Jaeger ponies of German origin, took such commodities as wool and hides from Settle to the lowland areas and returned with essential commodities like corn (from the east) and salt (from the west). In days when a good deal of meat was preserved for winter consumption, salt was in constant demand. It was obtained from the salt-pans of Lancashire and Cheshire.

The leading horse in a train was the 'bell horse', the bells on its harness giving warning to other users of the route. Wheeled traffic being uncommon, an excitedly chattering crowd would assemble at Settle on a September day in 1662, as a horse-drawn coach bearing Lady Anne Clifford drew up outside the inn where her Ladyship proposed to spend the night.

Lady Anne travelled in medieval splendour, with retinue—and, often, a special cart for her favourite bed. Having slept in Settle, she continued her journey 'over the moor to Mawham water Tarne, where I had not been 9 or 10 years before, and so into my own house at Barden Tower...'

John Ogilby's *Britannia* (1675), an early road-book, indicates a route down Kirkgate (the way to Giggleswick Church) with a river crossing at Settle Bridge. Ogilby mentioned 'a Stone Bridg' and referred to 'Gigleswick' as 'a village of 5 Furlongs extent and some Entertainment...' The exit was over that formidable hill, High Rigg, to Lawkland.

Even when the river bridge was available (and such a bridge existed as early as 1498), a ford was used by pack-horse trains as a short cut, avoiding a hill, the route crossing The Fellins on a paved way and passing near Armitstead Hall to rejoin the main highway near Beck House.

Duck Lane, a track leaving Settle market place to the south, led travellers to a river ford near Anley, beyond which lay the route to Rathmell and Clitheroe.

Market Days

IN 1708, Queen Anne granted Richard, Earl of Burlington, the right to hold additional markets at Settle, which had 'a convenient large square'.

The extra facilities were on the Tuesday before Palm Sunday

(cattle and all goods); April 15, or the Monday following (eggs); Tuesday after the feast of Pentecost (cattle and all goods); June 23, or the Monday following (lambs); October 12, or the Monday following (eggs), the Tuesday following October 16 (cattle and all goods); and Friday in any other week during three successive months commencing on the Friday before Easter Day (all manner of cattle).

Settle Market Place attracted itinerant entertainers. Samuel Watson, the Quaker, recorded on December 16, 1696: 'The word of the lord came upon me yesterday as a fire in my bosom, as I was walking in the market-place of Settle, and a heavenly command came upon me to bear witness against the wickedness set up in the people gathered and crowded together in a great concourse.'

His concern was over 'the lofty and highly set up sort of inchanters to evil call'd mountebanks who, capernaum-like, in their serpentine subtility, bewitch people with vain laughter, madness and folly, by their ungodly actings and lying wonders.' Watson was probably denouncing a small band of actors.

What did Samuel think of the local men who lost their inhibitions on Shrove Tuesday and played a turbulent, chaotic game of football in Kirkgate?

Daniel Defoe (1724) found Settle 'a much better town than we expected in such a country...Looking forward to the north-west of us we saw nothing but high mountains, which had a terrible aspect...especially Penigent Hill. So that having no manner of inclination to encounter them, merely for the sake of seeing a few villages and a parcel of wild people, we turned short northeast...'

It was not just a fear of mountains. A headless man was said to frequent the vicinity of Barker's Beck. The Scaleber Trash was a being which dragged clanking chains.

Work House Records

THE Settle Township Book, 'whearin is gott downe all disbursements concerning the towne and township of Settle', records [May 4, 1739] that Ruth Armistead 'has undertaken the care of the Work House as heretofore for the ensuing year at the rate of forty shillings.'

Thomas Newhouse, of Settle, undertook 'the care of the maintenance and labour of the persons in the above Work House' at a similar rate.

Servants of the Church

THE records of Giggleswick Church for 1736 indicate that the dog-whipper received five shillings a year 'for his pains'. The remuneration was raised to ten shillings a year in 1772 when John Higson agreed to take over the task of 'whiping the dogs out of the Church and keeping the doors shutt.'

The Clerk's pay in 1747 amounted to £1.15s.8d, which included 'washing linning, register writing, cleaning ye Church, taking care of ye clock, taking care of ye cloths, dressing ye plate, dressing ye leads, dressing ye grayte' and much else.

Attendance at Church was compulsory, which involved long journeys for some, the parish being far-flung. At one religious festival, there were so many communicants that ten gallons of wine were consumed.

Part-time Soldiers

UNDER an Act passed in 1757, each county had to provide a certain number of militiamen, each parish in turn being liable for its quota. The able-bodied were listed, and from names on the list the appropriate number was chosen by ballot.

The expense of equipping them was a parochial charge. Thus, in the Overseers' accounts at Settle, items totalling as much as £90 a year appear during the period of the Napoleonic War for 'militia and volunteer expenses'.

A man who was selected for service need not carry it out personally. He could avoid it by providing a substitute or by paying £10 for the purpose.

Market Tolls

THE Earl of Burlington, as lord of the manor, had a good income from market tolls on such goods as 'wheat, beans, barley, peas and oate meale (but chiefly oatemeale)... Every week quantitys of oate meale are bought at Settle Markett by persons living in the Dales and other parts of the Country, they growing little or noe grain in those places, being barren parts...'

Burlington leased to Thomas Chamberlaine of Skipton, gent., for four years 'all the tolls and customs of the fairs and markets of Settle and also the fairs of Long preston, together with all the usual stallages and dues for Green Hides and Seal of Leather and also the liberty of fishery in the Town of Giggleswick and River of Ribble...' The annual rent was £17.5s.

Settle's Market Cross was the point at which the Accession of a new monarch was proclaimed and [in the days of the Commonwealth] banns of marriage were called. In a cellar close to the Cross was the town gaol—a cellar where wrong-doers languished while awaiting to hear of their fate.

Settle was noted for its livestock. Cattle, sheep, even geese, were on sale on the appointed days. Geese were walked to market from the surrounding farms, their webbed feet reinforced against the roughness of the roads by a coverlet of tar, through which they had been persuaded to walk at the start of the journey.

The town became a noted marketing centre for leather, which was in constant demand for clothing, horse harness and saddles, boots and belting. Tan pits had been made at Langcliffe [a site now occupied by the church]; on the high road to Settle [in the vicinity of the beck]; in Upper Settle; at Catteral Hall and in the hamlet of Merebeck [between Settle and Long Preston].

Dealers attended the special markets from as far away as Dodworth Green, near Barnsley. They met in chattering groups at the *Talbot*, formerly known as *The Dog*. A 'talbot' was a fierce breed of dog associated with the Talbots of Bashall Hall, in Bowland.

Kept by the Parish

ON December 8, 1778 [as was noted in the Settle Township Book], Thomas Whittam, son of Widow Whittam, became one of the Poor Children who were put out as Parish Apprentices, for seven years. Thomas took up work with Christopher Clapham, of Clapham.

On September 22 in the following year, John Gawthrop fell by lot to become apprenticed to Widow Williams at her house in Duck Street. The Widow died three years later and John was subsequently returned to the care of the township. He went into service with Thomas Blackburn.

The Parish helped [1776] when Jane Shaw wanted to fit out her son 'for the Sea'. She was paid £2.13s.7d. The Parish appointed Elizabeth Clementson as a midwife [1786].

The Jurors dealing with Parish affairs sometimes met in private houses and at other times in public houses. Settle had an abundance of such places, including *Black Bull* (1778), *The Lamb, Duke of Devonshire, The Buck* and *Joiners' Arms*.

Paley of Giggleswick

IN 1744, William Paley began a long reign (55 years) at Giggleswick School, a period during which the income was vastly increased, which was also the case with the curriculum, now including mathematics, merchants' accounts and writing.

The Governors were persuaded (1795) to approve new Statutes giving more latitude in the organisation of the school and the reimbursement of its staff. The old schoolhouse was replaced by a larger building (1795) but an inscribed stone from the days of Carr the founder was retained.

The annual feast took place at Giggleswick on March 12, which was Potation Day to the scholars, who received gifts of figs, buns and ale. The Governors, masters and a few friends, dined at the *Hart's Head* and drank copious quantities of wine, rum, brandy, ale, porter and beer.

Ways with Wool

FOR centuries, woollen manufacture had been at a domestic level, the weaving and spinning taking place in farms and cottages.

Kendal and Halifax were old centres for woollen manufacture. At Kendal, wool from the fell sheep was coarsely spun into 'bump', which was then transported to centres in the nearby dales country to be distributed for knitting into stockings, gloves and jerseys.

Halifax depended greatly on the Craven Spinners—the farmers' wives who, especially in winter, could operate their large spinning wheels, which they turned by hand. The bobbin, revolving at high speed, gave the 'twist' while the spinner drew out the 'roving'. When the wheel was turned in the opposite direction, the thread was wound on to the bobbin.

Jonathan Akroyd, a clothier of Halifax, sent his combed wool by packhorse to farmsteads at Tosside, Wigglesworth, Austwick and

Dunsop Bridge. Agents distributed the wool to spinsters in the surrounding district. The wool was spun into yarn for one shilling a pound. When it was collected, a further supply of wool was made available.

Keighley to Kendal

IN the early part of the 18th century, the road through Settle was 'from the Narrowness thereof in many Places, and the Nature of the Soil, become very ruinous and in great Decay, and is not only almost impassable by Wheel Carriages, but very dangerous to travellers. . .'

Repairs to the road were carried out through the efforts of people living beside it. They were supposed to give their labour on six days a year and to provide horses and carts for the jobs in hand.

In 1753, during the reign of George II, an Act of Parliament was secured for repairing, constructing, amending and widening a Turnpike road from Keighley to Kendal.

The money was raised by contributions from local trustees, who would be reimbursed from tolls paid by road users. The qualification was having land of an annual value of £100 or property worth £3,000. A Trustee was forbidden to make any profit from his association with the Turnpike.

The first meetings were held at 'the dwellinghouse of Robert Johnson in Settle'. Among those who gave their name to the enterprise were Birkbeck (Anley), Farrer (Ingleborough Hall) and Ingleby (Lawkland Hall).

Thomas Carr, of Paley Green, became the clerk and treasurer at fifteen guineas per annum. Stephen Knowles, of Newby, was appointed surveyor from Settle Bridge to Kirkby in Kendal [presumably Kirkby Lonsdale] and William Carr of Langcliffe from Settle to Keighley, each at a salary of £20 per annum.

Only one gift of land was made, the donor being Josias Morley, of Giggleswick. John Alcock and Francis Cripps, of Skipton, each offered a loan at four and a-half per cent to be secured by the toll fees.

In 1753, the Giggleswick and Lawkland stretch of the old road, which included High Rigg, was vacated in favour of an improved Back Lane, an old route from the top of Belle Hill to the limeworks and on beside Giggleswick Scar [then known as 'Brayshaw Scar'] to Brunton and Rawlinshaw.

The width of the new roadway was to be seven yards, of which five yards were to be maintained as a metalled track. The main toll gate was a large structure which, when not in use, was kept padlocked. There was a smaller gate with a bolt which was operated from within the toll-house.

Joshua Parsons, a mason of Newton-in-Bowland, contracted to repair or construct this stretch of road for £105 per measured mile. A toll-house at Long Preston bridge was ordered at a cost of £41, 'the house to be slated, the timber and wood in house gate and rails to be good oak, except chamber floor good ash.'

Settle Bridge, one of those repairable by the West Riding, was stated in The Book of Bridges to be 'a very good stone Bridge with 2 ribb'd Arches, founded on a Rock'. The road from here to the top of Belle Hill was widened in 1755, the bridge itself being widened in 1783.

The effect of this re-aligning of the main road was to by-pass Giggleswick. The owner of the *Hart's Head* in Belle Hill promptly closed it as an inn and built more capacious premises beside the new road.

At Settle, the town was, in effect, turned on its axis, being re-aligned from north to south. The moorland crossing from Long Preston to Upper Settle was succeeded by a new stretch at lower level, entering the town at Duck Street, which was re-named Duke

Street. A redundant milestone from the old highway was built into a wall on School Hill.

The enterprising owner of the *Golden Lion* closed down the premises in Cheapside and opened up round the corner, to intercept the Turnpike traffic. Peter Watson, as 'mine host', was soon welcoming strangers who arrived by coach, including the Hon. Mrs Murray Aust, who found the bedrooms were 'middling' and the parlour very good.

The maximum toll for travellers using the whole road were: For every coach, chariot, berlin, landau, phaeton, chaise, chair, hearse or litter, drawn by six horses or more, the sum of 7s.6d. Drawn by five horses, 5s; two horses, 3s.4d; and one horse, 2s.

For every waggon, wain, cart or other carriage, drawn by six horses or beasts of draught, 20s; for five or four horses or beasts of draught, 5s, for three or two ditto, 3s.4d; for one horse or beast of draught, 1s.6d.

For every horse, mare gelding, mule or ass, laden or unladen, and not drawing, the sum of 5d. For every drove of oxen or neat cattle, the sum of 2s per score, or so in proportion for any greater or less number. For every drove of calves, hogs, sheep or lambs, the sum of one shilling per score, and so in proportion for any greater or less number.

Trying to avoid a toll gate by making a wide sweep was now a local pastime. When 'Mr ffountaine' was charged (1753) with 'bilking' the Turnpike at Clapham', he confessed the fault and promised to pay the toll to prevent process.

Jonathan Chadock was prosecuted (1774) for sneaking through the toll-keeper's back garden with a horse and thus defrauding the Turnpike.

Dodging work was in favour with such as John Armistead, George Clough and John Beaumont of Lawkland. They were contacted by the Clerk of the Trustees (1754) to appear and show cause why they neglected to perform their two days' statute work upon the Turnpike Road.

James Wilman was paid two shillings (in 1754) for '2 men and 2 horses, half a day's leading stones.' John Bradley (1794) was paid £2.0.9d for damage to his lands in getting road mending material between Rawlinshaw and Cross o' th' Streets.

On November 4, 1758, the Trustees decided to erect a toll-house at Lobley Lane End [Stackhouse road end] 'about as near as can be computed 200 yards west of Settle Bridge'.

When, in autumn, the droves of Scottish cattle followed a traditional route down the dale from Gearstones they avoided the toll bar by using the high road from Langcliffe to Settle, entering the town at the head of Constitution Hill.

Thomas Jefferys' map of the County of York (1771) indicates the use of Banks Lane at the start of a route leading up the dale, via Stainforth and Horton. It was also the start of a route on to Malham Moor, reached in the vicinity of Capon Hall.

Visitors consulting the map would be deterred from climbing Ingleborough and Whernside by the height quoted—each being 1,760 yards, with the height of Penyghent given as 1,740 yards.

In the 1750s, Settle had a Duke as Lord of the Manor when Lord Hartington married the heiress of the last Earl of Cork and Burlington and became Duke of Devonshire.

The inn with a regal name, *Royal Oak,* was sold by Sarah Dixon and Joseph Bell to Francis Staniforth for £300. The 17th century inn, associated with the Cookson family, who at that time owned all the property on the western side of the market place, had been rebuilt half a century earlier.

In 1780 attempts were made to raise money for constructing a canal from Lancaster to Settle, via Ingleton, with a great tunnel under Huntworth. The prospectus mentioned the buoyancy of local trade—the quarrying for gritstone suitable for building; the inexhaustible quarries of blue-flags, grit-flags, excellent blue slate, and grit-slate.

Also referred to were the great quantities of goods and merchandise then passing 'by land carriage, at a very great expense, from London, Hull, Sheffield, Leeds, Halifax, &c., through Settle to Kendal.'

In the later part of the 18th century, Settle was one of the Dales towns noted for its clockmakers, the best-known family being Hargraves. William Hargraves's skill was such he made a clock which, at four-hourly intervals, played two verses of a hymn tune [on six bells] before striking the hour.

His son, Thomas, was also a clock-maker and, like his father, a Quaker. He was expelled from the fraternity because he selected a non-Quaker wife, Sarah, daughter of John Sergeantson, who was a wool-comber. The marriage ceremony took place at Giggleswick Church in 1764.

War on Want

WITH a protracted war against the French in progress, an increase in poverty and unemployment was experienced.

Those responsible for the Workhouse had to exercise the utmost economy to make the funds last out. It was decided that any pauper who moved from one township to another must have a certificate from his previous residence which absolved the new township against liability to maintain him or her.

The first Workhouse was in use from 1739 until 1759, when more commodious accommodation was found in two houses, a barn and two gardens in Upper Settle, leased to the town for 21 years at £4 per annum.

When the administration of the Poor Law was revised in 1773, two unpaid Overseers were appointed for Settle. Four years later,

John Hodgson was appointed as Overseer and Constable at Settle for a year, the remuneration being seven guineas. [Hodgson eventually gave up the job of Constable but remained an Overseer for 17 years].

The First Tourists

THE word travel is derived from 'travail', which is Norman French for labour. Travel, once an onerous business, was now being undertaken for pleasure by a few 'gentlemen of taste and leisure'.

During the later part of the 18th century, the so-called Romantic period developed. For some, it was a quest for Sublimity, but Romanticism was also, in truth, a revolt against Classicism, which had long dominated art, literature, music and architecture and had become somewhat sterile.

In addition, war with the French had prevented the well-to-do from making the Grand Tour. Some of them, reading accounts of travels in the wilder parts of Britain, emulated the writers and developed a love-hate relationship with the landscape.

The first tourists at Settle and Giggleswick associated this limestone country of Caves, Crags and Chasms with the Lake District. What better, after experiencing the awesome, terrible mountains of Cumbria than to 'take in' the natural curiosities of High Craven?

An early tourist-writer, the poet Thomas Gray, was in the district in 1769. Heading southwards, he descended 'Brunton Brow' into 'a chearful valley (though thin of trees) to Giggleswick, a village with a small piece of water by its side [the Tarn], covered with coot'. This lay 'near to a church which belongs also to Settle.'

Half a mile further, having passed the Ribble over a bridge, Mr Gray arrived at Settle, 'a small market town standing directly under a rocky fell; there are not in it above a dozen good-looking houses, the rest are old and low, with little wooden porticos in front.'

The inn he selected 'pleased me much (though small) for the neatness and civility of the good woman that kept it: so I lay there two nights and went to visit the Gordale Scar. . .'

Thomas Pennant, antiquary and botanist, visiting Settle in 1773, found himself standing 'at the foot of a monstrous limestone rock, called Castleberg, which threatens destruction'. Settle exactly resembled 'a shabby French town with a place in the middle.'

Settle was then the resort of numbers of coiners and filers [who clipped pieces off gold coins of the realm, selling the gold]. These men were now idle 'by reason of the recent salutary law respecting the weight of gold.'

The Rev John Hutton, of Burton in Kendal, after visiting the district in 1779, wrote *Tour to the Caves* [published in 1781]. He conveyed his excitement at going underground in natural shafts and caves; he also looked at the landscape with a scientist's eye and rightly deduced from fossil evidence that the limestone had a marine origin.

He, poor man, being a cleric, was left trying to reconcile the evidence of his eyes with the Biblical story of the Flood.

Hutton did look round Settle, a town which was 'irregularly built' with 'not many good houses in it.' The church was at Giggleswick, 'which appeared to be the court end of the parish.'

Commercial Affairs

SETTLE replaced its venerable market cross in 1784 as though to mark an upward turn in its commercial life. Hides were being dressed in town. Settle leather was famous.

William Hoole, an eminent tanner, set off on horseback to attend Settle Fair in 1785. He got no further than Bradford, where his horse threw him. William, badly bruised, 'expired soon after.'

Towards the end of the century, Cragdale was built by John Peart, a member of an old Grassington family who developed a solicitor's practice at Settle. Ashfield, across the road, was built by William Birkbeck (1772-1838).

Men and Machines

TOWARDS the end of the 18th century, textile processes were mechanised as the result of a series of brilliant inventions. In North Ribblesdale, old corn mills were transformed into cotton mills.

In 1783, Langcliffe High Mill was adapted for cotton spinning by three Lancashire men—George and William Clayton and R Walshman (their brother-in-law). They already had a large cotton mill in Keighley.

High Mill, Langcliffe, in 1848

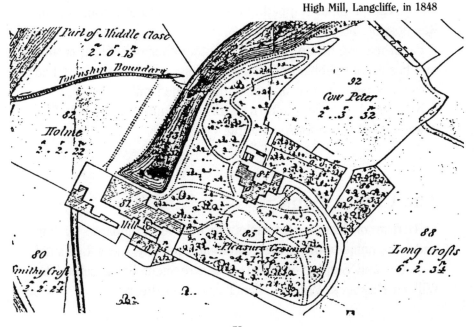

The site of the High Mill is historic. Here stood a monastic corn mill, followed by a corn mill used until about the year 1650. The premises reconstructed and extended by the partners in 1783 created the second cotton spinning mill in Yorkshire.

For the work, local ashlar was used, plus lime from lower Ribblesdale, lead from Grassington, and iron from the forges of Lancaster and Caton. The slate needed for roofing purposes came by canal to Holme Bridge at Gargrave and was then carted along the Turnpike to Settle.

The Shed (between Langcliffe and Settle) was built for weaving. Bridge End Mill, at Settle, became a cotton spinning mill occupied, from 1785 until 1795, by Wilkinson Buck Jay & Company. The mill, a free standing building set at right angles to the Ribble, straddles the tail race from an external water wheel made of iron—cast iron, wrought iron and sheet iron (for the buckets).

A novel attempt was made to ventilate the buckets by cutting four slots on each section and fitting leather flap valves to allow for the escape of air trapped in the buckets so that a complete fill was possible at every revolution.

Paper-making began in 1793, using another old mill, this time one beside the Ribble between Langcliffe and Stainforth. It had previously been a corn mill and then a snuff mill.

King's Mill had been, in turn, a corn mill and a snuff mill before it was devoted to cotton spinning.

The Craven Bank

THE firm of Messrs Birkbecks, Alcocks & Company, trading under the name of the Craven Banking Company, was established at Settle and Skipton in 1791, the agreement being signed by William Birkbeck, William Alcock and John Peart.

The Birkbecks, who were to become the most notable of the local families, commenced business about the end of the seventeenth century in a general retail shop, prospering to the extent of employing about 200 in a wool combing business alone. The wool was put out to local homes for spinning. It was truly a 'cottage industry'.

Towards the end of the eighteenth century, the family bought the Giggleswick corn mill, being keen to get the water rights. They improved the waterwheel and converted the premises into a spinning mill.

In 1794, the Birkbecks were at Skipton, where they opened a warehouse to handle the 3,000 packs of wool a year. The wool was stored here pending the sorting, combing and the spinning of the wool at the family mills in Linton and Addingham. It was subsequently made into 'stuffs, viz shalloons, calimancoes, and all sorts of durable goods.'

The combination of merchants and lawyers was a happy one for the Craven Bank. *The Gentlemen's Magazine* [1838] published the obituary of William Birkbeck, 'banker, of Settle', observing that he was a member of the Society of Friends who qualified as a Justice of the Peace. 'He was courteous and gentle in his transactions with all, faithful in the discharge of his duties, and persevering almost to a proverb.'

The high esteem in which the partners were held meant that Craven notes were in good repute, and were always well received, being in many cases preferred to Bank of England notes.

These local businessmen hit on the ingenious idea of obtaining the goodwill of the Craven farmers by adopting the engraving of a cow on the notes. If a choice of notes was offered to a farmer, he was inclined to say: 'Gie me one wi' a coo on.'

Diversion and Enclosure

IN 1792, the Turnpike trustees greatly improved the main road through Settle district, opening a new stretch at Cave Ha' which avoided the high road by Brunton House and the steep hill at Rawlinshaw. The new road took a lower course under the limestone crag to a field of Mr Clapham's 'and thence under Crow Nest Scarr'.

Travellers from Long Preston to Settle beheld a marshy valley standing in water. The wet nature of the ground was indicated by old Norse names—Bigholme (low lying ground by a stream), Sourdales (from saurr, dirty or marshy, and deill, a portion of a common field). Cracoe Mire came from kraka (crow) and myrrr (swampy ground).

In 1799, an Act of Parliament was obtained for 'dividing and inclosing several Open Fields and Stinted Pastures within the Township of Longpreston in the West Riding of the County of York, and for Embanking and Draining several Parcels of Ground within the same Township called Longpreston Ings'.

Enclosure awards are commonplace; much rarer is one with clauses relating to the drainage of the lower ground. At Long Preston ings, fifteen open and unenclosed fields are specified; they contained about 150 acres, plus four undivided unstinted pastures 'containing together by estimation Four Hundred Acres or thereabouts...'

Experience led to the construction of earthen banks of such a height that only exceptional floods overtopped them. Higher up the valley, banks made by local farmers were five feet high in places.

The scheme incorporated a Cut, or open drain across the fields. Flagged bridges allowed for the passage of horse-drawn carts. Flagstone, for bridges and other construction work, was quarried on Hunter Bark, above Settle.

Settle and Giggleswick

ONLY the Ribble separated the two communities of Settle and Giggleswick yet their evolution had differed greatly. John Houseman, an 18th century visitor to North Ribblesdale, commented on those differences.

Settle, which stood in the shelter of 'rocky hills', had become 'an inconsiderable market town'. Giggleswick was the setting for the parish church, 'near to which the gentry have erected very neat boxes' and formed 'a kind of separation from the tradesmen'.

The area was self-reliant. Some local occupations of 1803 were cooper, mercer, tallow chandler, grazier, hatter, roper, nailer, ostler, attorney-at-law, skinner, clockmaker, farrier, chaise-driver, clogger, piece maker, currier, warper, paper-maker, porter, linen draper, miller.

Settle had its lime-burners, who operated a kiln at the base of Castleberg, from which they obtained their stone. The inhabitants had the lime-burner presented at the court of the Lord of the Manor, 'fearing that if any more was dug out, the rock might fall and bury the whole town in ruins...'

Twelve wise and just men were impanelled as jurers and sent to view this impending nuisance; the verdict they returned was that if ever it fell, 'it would tumble not towards the town, but the direct or contrary way.'

Changing Scene

DURING the later part of the 17th century, the impetus to enclose the common fields in the interests of new methods of agriculture led to Enclosure Acts and the transformation of the landscape by a pattern of drystone walls.

The promoters of enclosure schemes did well; the common

man, as usual, fared badly, in this case losing his right of pasturage on the common land.

The Act for enclosing Settle Banks, High Scarr and Scaleber was passed in 1758. That for dividing the stinted pastures in Langcliffe [Cow Close, Over Close, Langcliffe Scar, Dawshaw, Winskill Stones and Gorbeck] was approved in 1789.

Changes in Settle

THE first Methodist Chapel (1796) gave its name to Chapel Street. The Congregationalists had some initial opposition from the Methodists, but soon became 'peaceable', and established their chapel (Zion) in 1816.

From 1822, the *Union* coach service through Settle to Kendal and Leeds was augmented by a twice-a-week coach service to Manchester. By 1840, coaches were operating daily to Skipton, Lancaster and Kirkby Lonsdale.

William Birkbeck, the banker, who had built Ashfield in Duke Street, landscaped an area extending to Bond Lane, where a pretty lodge was built. William enjoyed organising parties. The spaciousness of Ashfield, both within and at the rear, made it ideal for such gatherings.

Mrs Birkbeck had been Rachel Gough, sister of Charles Gough, who died in grim weather on Helvellyn, in the Lake District. His dog remained with the body for weeks on end. The incident was immortalised in a poem written by Wordsworth.

Among the captains of industry were the Procters, who operated from Anley Mill. The premises were lost by fire in August, 1825. Paley the diarist wrote:

'One of the engines called a 'Devil'. . .took fire from friction and there was so much cotton hanging and lying about that it spread with such rapidity that the whole was burnt down in about an hour.'

Soon, the Procters were back in the cotton business at King's Mill. Procter's Row, a terrace of small stone cottages, is named after the mill-owning family.

Giggleswick Tax-payers

AT the turn of the century, the gentry who lived in the 'very neat boxes' near the parish church, were taxed according to their life-style. Tax was claimed on such diverse items as windows, male servants, saddle horses—even dogs.

An example was the £26.9.4d paid by Jane Backhouse, the sum being assessed on 26 windows, house duty, a male servant, four-wheeled carriage, two horses (saddle), one horse (cart) and a dog, the latter costing her 4s.

Hopefully, they did not get a whiff of smoke from the small lime-kilns which had appeared alongside Giggleswick Scar. Edmund Brown, one of the burners in 1805, was reported to the Turnpike trustees because his kiln and others were so near the road as to be a nuisance.

Edmund was alleged to be 'getting and throwing stones on the turnpike for supplying the kilns, the same kilns being at the foot of very high ground.' He was inducted at York Assizes and agreed to remove kilns and construct a wall.

Writer and Artist

THE painter Edward Dayes (1803) wrote of Settle as being 'situated in the midst of barren hills'. The town was romantic, 'the houses being the most whimsical, picturesque and odd anywhere to be met with...The market place in particular had to me the strangest effect imaginable...

'Full in the light appeared the market house, raised on an

arcade, above which, in a gallery that leads to different dwellings, were seen various people, busily employed in humble occupations.

'Add to the whole, by way of back-ground, a tremendous cliff, 300 feet high, which impends fearfully over the back of the town, in the most terrific manner, and some idea of the scene may be formed.'

Travellers who arrived from the north in 1804 found a new stretch of road along the line of an old footpath between the Church and Settle Bridge. As a path, it had been referred to in 1680, when the Court Leet ordered a fine of 3s.4d against anyone who rode 'of the Northfield being the Church footway between Settle and Giggleswick Bridge'.

The land for this improvement had been purchased for £200 a statute acre. The new road, which cost £2.7s.6d a rood, was 13 yards 'between the fences', ten yards having been stoned and the crown having a thickness of fourteen inches. The whole had been covered with two inches of good gravel.

Coaching Inns

EARLY in the 19th century, the three most notable inns at Settle and Giggleswick were the *Spreadeagle* (Kirkgate), *Golden Lion* (Duke Street) and the *Hart's Head* (Giggleswick). From 1822, Settle was the starting point of a twice-a-week coach service to Manchester.

The *Spreadeagle,* a tall, stylish building on the north side of Kirkgate, had been created by Thomas Procter, a Settle cooper, who in 1734 bought a cluster of buildings and converted them into the inn.

The 'old' *Golden Lion,* which stood in Cheapside, was mentioned in a document of 1654. The 'new' *Golden Lion* was opened in Duke Street to take advantage of the re-routed traffic following the opening of the turnpike, in 1753, and the first landlord was Peter Watson.

The 'old' *Hart's Head,* down Belle Hill, was owned by the Garsdale family, who closed it on the coming of the turnpike road and opened up a commodious 'new' *Hart's Head* beside the road.

The *Royal Oak,* established in 1689, was rebuilt about 1720 and enlarged in mid-century to take advantage of the Turnpike traffic.

Settle Market Day around 1820

Hall for the Town

THE shambling form of the Old Tollbooth did not seem to reflect the new spirit of the town.

This Tollbooth, centuries old, had a high-pitched roof, covered with stone slabs. The lower storey consisted of shops, a room for the Watchman and the town lock-up, with a dungeon underneath. The Watchman, who patrolled the town with horn lantern and rattle in hand, called out the hour of the night—as near as he could give it!

The upper storey was reached by three flights of outside steps. A balcony or gallery ran round the building, forming a platform from which the Town Crier made his announcements. Living quarters for several families were situated at the corners of the building.

The centre of the upper floor held the Pig Jury Room, in which the town's business was transacted and where were kept the standard brass measures, for a peck, half peck and fourthpart.

The Tollbooth made the town look shabby; it must go and be replaced by something more imposing. So it was demolished in about 1830 and the site used for the present Town Hall.

The *Leeds Mercury* for September 14, 1833, noted that this new public meeting included a market-house, newsroom, public library and savings bank. The Hall would be 'a decided ornament to the town and neighbourhood'.

Settle in 1834

THE Birkbecks' new mansion at Anley was completed in 1818. From its windows could be seen parkland extending to the Ribble.

Settle, as noted in *Kelly's Directory* (1834), was 'a small well-built market town...singular & picturesque...the town being seated at the foot of Castlebergh, a conical lime-stone rock, 210 feet high, backed by a cluster of rugged crags.'

The compiler of *Kelly's* mentioned Settle's 'most striking peculiarity—the prevalence of stone fences in the neighbourhood; these, in the opinion of some, detract from the beauty of the surrounding country. Others deem them more consistent with its character than hawthorn hedges.'

The Settle under review was the liveliest part of an extensive parish with a total of 3,017 inhabitants.

The 'gentry and clergy' included Thomas and William Birkbeck at Anley; the Misses Mary and Elizabeth Dawson of Marshfield House; Mrs Swale at Langcliffe Hall and, in the immediate countryside, John Geldard at Cappleside, John Yorke at Halton Place and Thomas Ingleby at Lawkland Hall.

John Gibbins, as Postmaster, presided over a service which received letters from London, Leeds and Kirkby Lonsdale each morning at seven and despatched any outgoing mail every afternoon at four. Letters from Lancaster and Clapham arrived (by foot-post) every afternoon at two, and were despatched every morning at half past seven.

Banking business was conducted through Birkbecks, Alcocks & Peart and presiding over the day-to-day affairs of the Savings Bank, as secretary, was John Tatham, jnr.

The Settle area had nine blacksmiths, fifteen boot and shoe markers, six braziers and tinmen, ten butchers, two clog and patten makers, seven grocers and tea dealers.

Among the miscellaneous occupations were those of nail maker (John Baldwin), horse dealer (John Bowskill), cattle dealer (Thomas Bowskill), cooper (Richard Broughton), lime burner (Thomas Clark), hair dresser (William Cork), retailer of beer (Charles Duckett), distributer of stamps (Rd Redmayne), hat manufacturer (William Turner) and printer (William Walker).

At Giggleswick, *Kelly's* made special mention of 'a free grammar school, founded by Edward VI' and 'a very ancient parish church, dedicated to St Alkald'.

Lord of Settle

THE Duke of Devonshire, as lord of the manor of Settle, gave the town distinction. The Duke's representative held Courts Baron twice a year, and a Constable was appointed.

His Grace drew tolls for a variety of sources, examples being the sale of a new hat [one halfpenny] and cattle sold in the market [fourpence a score]. The last Pinder and Toll Collector was Robert Hartley.

No longer were the Duke's rights proclaimed annually, as in ancient time, when representatives of Settle with javelins 'rode the boundary'. The town became one of the 'stations' named in the new Boundary Act (an appendage to the Reform Bill) for receiving votes at the election of members to represent the West Riding of the county.

Gossip was spread across the district by the passengers of coaches stopping at the posting houses for refreshment and a change of horses. In 1826, the heiress Ellen Turner was abducted and, on the way to Gretna Green, the party drove north via Skipton (staying overnight at the *Devonshire Hotel*) and Settle (taking refreshments at the *Golden Lion*) and Kirkby Lonsdale (*Rose and Crown*).

At Settle, posting horses were let to travellers for the next stage (Skipton or Kirkby Lonsdale), the charge ranging from 1s to 1s.6d a mile. The horses were returned when someone was travelling in the opposite direction.

By the Ribble

THE 1830s were marred by the destruction through fire of the snuff mill [King's Mill], which the Procters re-built.

From 1830 until 1865, no weirs existed at Settle and Langcliffe and so the migratory salmon could reach the gravel beds at the head of the Ribble for spawning. In 1834, a party of poachers killed 400 salmon. The roe of the fish, when potted, was sold for £20.

A Union Workhouse was established on the Giggleswick side of the river in 1834. The Poor Law Amendment Act had provided for several townships and parishes to be grouped. By 1841 the Workhouse had 180 inmates.

Adult Education

IN town, a Mechanics' Institute of the type promoted by a Settle man, Dr George Birkbeck, was founded in 1831 along the lines of those which were firmly associated with his name.

Birkbeck, who was born in 1776 and educated at Settle and Edinburgh, qualified as a doctor and worked in Glasgow and then London. The Mechanics' Institutes were for 'men who worked with their hands' who wished to improve their education by attending evening classes.

Birkbeck died in 1841 and was not to see the devastating effects of trade recession. The 1840s were to be known as The Hungry Forties. Trade was slack and working class families merely subsisted.

Langcliffe High Mill closed down. Almost every house in the village was empty as people emigrated, many of them to Lancashire. A district of Accrington became known as 'Little Langcliffe'.

A New Church

WHEN Holy Ascension was opened at Settle in 1838, it was the first new Anglican church to have been consecrated in Craven for three centuries.

A proposal to build a church had been put forward in 1835, Mr Wilkinson of Hellifield and Mr Tennant of Riddings and their sisters offering £500 towards a building. Mr Wilkinson said he would donate a site in Upper Settle.

At a public meeting, presided over by the Rev Rowland Ingram, Headmaster of Giggleswick School, a subscription list was opened and handsome donations received from the Misses Dawson of Marshfield, Mrs Swale of Langcliffe Hall, the Rev John Dawson,

Vicar of Giggleswick, Thomas Clapham, John Peart and the Craven Bank.

Mr Ingram laid the foundation stone of the new building on June 15, 1836. The site chosen was beside the main road, below the mini-mansion of Townhead, which then was the home of William Bolland; he became one of the first trustees.

The style used for the new Church was Early English, from designs by Thomas Richman. A building capable of seating 600 people was constructed at a cost of about £3,000, a sum which was more than covered by subscriptions. Mrs Swale had donated £1,000.

The first vicar of Holy Ascension was a 39 year old Kendalian, the Rev Hogarth John Swale, instituted on February 16, 1839. He left Settle in 1848 but returned to the town after serving for nine years as chaplain to the British Embassy in Paris. His retirement home, Ingfield, had been built at his instructions in 1842.

Social Occasions

AMONG the diversions for men, between 1820 and 1850, were meetings of the Settle Oyster Club at the *Golden Lion.* The association of an inland town with an oyster is apparent from a much used quotation:

> *Then the world's mine oyster,*
> *Which with my sword I'll open.*

A Club broadsheet had a short life but a merry one in the 1840s. One issue included foreign intelligence from the 'western dependencies of Slaidburn and Austwick' and a City article in which it was reported: 'There is very little doing...Bank of England notes are selling as waste paper at 4d a lb.'

Such diversions as the Oyster Club helped to shorten the winter in North Ribblesdale.

School Life

FROM 1782 until 1839, the Vicar of Giggleswick was the Rev John Clapham, known as 'the sporting parson'. During his incumbency, the parish was overtaken by the industrial revolution and he played a leading role in educational changes, not least the establishment of elementary schools at Giggleswick, Settle and Langcliffe.

The Settle National Schools opened on part of the site occupied by the *Spreadeagle* Hotel in Kirkgate in 1816 or 1817, providing elementary day and Sunday education for the children of the township. This school had strong Anglican associations. The Wesleyan Methodists had opened a Sunday School in 1809.

Subsequently, there was no rancour between Methodists and Anglicans. 'For some years, scholars of the Methodist Sunday School marched every Sunday morning to Giggleswick Church to say their catechism.'

The National Schools project had some worthy champions: the Rev John Clapham, Vicar of Giggleswick; his brother-in-law John Peart, who was a partner in the Craven Bank and had also donated the site [valued at £90], the Rev Roland Ingram, Master of Giggleswick Grammar School, John Hartley, a solicitor, and William Bolland.

A contemporary account relates: 'The roof is slated with grey slates and hipped at one end: the materials within are of excellent fine timber and the floor is flagged with good grit stone.'

According to the formula adopted by the National Society [which promoted and gave grants to such schools] the space adequate for one child was six square feet; the managers calculated that, based on this, the Schoolroom would hold 190 scholars, 120 boys and 70 girls.'

The number of children attending increased to such an extent that a room in the Folly was rented for the teaching of the girls. By 1849, the register held a total of over 200 children.

A Schoolmaster's Diary

GIGGLESWICK had a diarist in William Lodge Paley (1785-1847), who was the headmaster of Giggleswick National School for 27 years. The boys called him Old Putty Legs, but not to his face. Paley was also a bookseller and accountant.

Paley, having heard the Rev R Tomlinson preach at Giggleswick Church, confided in his diary that the cleric 'inforced the necessity of being religious and expatiated upon the comforts of being so. His manner of reading is rather too hasty but sufficiently loud.'

When the diary opened in September, 1814, he was recovering from a cold. That same month, the school was closed by an outbreak of scarlet fever which claimed several chidren.

When visiting the mill where he 'kept the books', Paley now smoked his pipe as a precaution against being infected, as well as for pleasure.

In early October, Paley related how five doctors were in attendance at Giggleswick when Robert Lister, who had endured the pain from 'a white swelling' in his knee, had his leg amputated without the benefit of anaesthetic.

In April, 1821, Wm Calvert slaughtered a very fat ox which had been fed by Mr King, of Austwick. The beast was 30 stone per qr. and contained 264 lb of tallow.

On Easter Day, many people 'took liquors' to the Ebbing and Flowing Well and returned drunk. 'How Lamentably depraved we are!'

On receiving six month's salary 'in a draft and 3 sovereigns—the latter a new gold coin, the first I have had', he paid Mr Waller [of the *Black Horse*] half a year's board.

This was not just a record of happenings. Paley wrote about his feelings. In October, 1824, he was 'so teased with teaching that my soul feels heaviness and my spirits dullness.' In May, 1827, 'vegitation [sic] has begun to luxuriate and I have slept twice without nightgown.'

Boom and Bust

THE decline of Settle's leather and hides industry came at a time when inventions in textiles had led to the establishment of large power-driven mills. In the first half of the 19th century, the population of Settle almost doubled.

By 1833 over 300 people were employed in the two largest mills in Giggleswick parish. These were Langcliffe High Mill [William Clayton and Sons] and King's Mill, Settle [John Proctor and Sons]. It was a period when the child worker formed part of the system and received (on average) 2s a week.

As industrialisation gained momentum, less was heard of the 'clack and shutter' of the domestic handloom, which had provided broad-based employment. Now the mill worker's well-being was linked with the entrepreneurial flair of a few individuals [leading, by mid-century, as related, to the closure of mills and migration of workers].

Township Finances

THE Rate Book of the Township of Settle (1843) indicates there were assessments on January 5 at the rate of 10d in the £ and on April 8 at 8d in the £ [the rate being levied four times a year]. The Rateable Value for both January and April was £8,060.15s.0¾d.

The Declaration as to accuracy of the document was signed in the January by John Birkbeck, jnr., and William Howson as Overseers, with James Ellison, who was a Churchwarden. The

Assessments were certified and allowed by William Clayton and Thomas Birkbeck, Justices of the Peace.

The April lists were confirmed by Silvester C Cork and James Brennand (as Overseers), James Ellison (Churchwarden), with William Clayton and Thomas Birkbeck (Magistrates). The Assistant Overseer was Henry King, jnr.

The Rate Book tells who owned the various properties and businesses. Robert Atkinson was at the *Spreadeagle;* he had buildings, cottages and land at Ling Copies, also renting 'Goldlands' and a barn from Thomas Birkbeck. George Hartley owned land and mill at Scaleber occupied by Thomas Brennand.

William Clayton owned the mill and cottages at Bridge End. Miss Dawson owned and occupied Marshfield House. Miss Lambert owned Cleatop and David Dale occupied the house. Stephen Wilman owned and John Harrison occupied the *Talbot.*

Isabella Hartley owned and occupied the *Golden Lion* and 'Dram Shop'. William Calvert had the title deeds for the *Naked Man,* which was occupied by Eli Harger. Joseph Harger, tenant at the *Royal Oak* [owned by George Hartley] also farmed the Lodge Estate under Thomas Ray.

The Shambles was owned by William Charnley. Shops and cellars were then occupied by butchers.

Stephen Hargreaves farmed on a grand scale. He rented Stockdale from Thomas Clapham, Great High Hill from William Dawson, Attermire from John Foster and was the tenant of several other fields.

Charles Ratcliffe owned and occupied a weaving shop in Upper Settle. Alice Thornber & Son owned and occupied the mill and cottages at Runley Bridge.

The Iron Road

THE first through rail service between the West Riding and the Lancashire coast, where holiday resorts were developing rapidly, was that known as the 'Little' North Western Railway, extending from Morecambe to Skipton. Here it connected with the Leeds-Bradford system.

The first sod was cut near Cleatop on December 31, 1846, by George William Frederick Howard, 7th Earl of Carlisle. The Castle

The 7th Earl of Carlisle (courtesy of Castle Howard)

Howard Archives contain his impressions of the day's events, as noted in his diary:

'I began the day with sore throat, headache & indigestion; then a procession in carriages to Cleatop where I was to dig the 1st sod of the North Western Railway—that is the line originally called, which is to go from Skipton to the Lancaster & Carlisle.

'It was a spot with a fine view & there were great numbers of people. Mr Wignoles (?) the Engineer dressed himself as a Navvy & gave me a beautiful spade to operate with. I had to take off great coat & to put on a Navvy's red worsted cap; I proceeded to dig,

71

but tho' the snow has disappeared west of leeds, & it was then a slight drizzle, I found the ground still hard enough from the frost to make it quite hard work, & I made but a bad Georgical attempt.

'I had then to make an harangue, still Coatless, & then to trundle off the wheelbarrow & empty my load, after Galtener then dug, & then the regular gang of workmen set to, who made a very different piece of work of it. I never saw a finer set of men.

'There was a very good prayer at the beginning. We returned to the Town & had a dinner of about 80 at the Golden Lion, the sonatery part of this proceeding was so steaming with wet that my coat was wet through. Mr Pudsey Dawner [Dawson]. of Hornby Castle, Chairman of the line, was so of the Dinner too. It passed off extremely well...'

In 1848, a survey was made of the locality. This 'freezes' the Settle area just before the transport revolution occurred.

Dog Kennel Mill [where now there are allotments—dogs not admitted!] stood down a short lane from the high road to Long Preston, not far from the Tannery. Near King's Mill a gasometer is marked.

The stream through Giggleswick is named Thames Beck and there is a Thames House. The church is shown as St Alkald's. Two houses named [where the present range of school buildings is to be seen] are Craven Bank and Holy Well.

In 1848, no road existed from Brackenber lane up to Close House. The old way from Giggleswick appears to have been from opposite the present Giggleswick School by 'Dalicar Lane', across fields to join an old road to Close House.

Tan pits are shown near Langcliffe School, where in due course an Anglican church was built.

The beck running by Giggleswick station was then known as Carr Beck. Rome was clearly marked. So was 'Farther' Rome, which then was in ruins. Kettlesbeck had a flour mill. [The miller named Dilworth died when he was caught in his wheel and soon afterwards the mill was pulled down].

In 1848, the first temporary railway station was called Lane Side Station, being indicated on the survey by a signal lamp and platform. The road leading from the new railway bridge towards Harden Bridge is marked Fummerber.

When the North Western Railway Company provided a station at Giggleswick and a regular service between Skipton and Lancaster, a local poet celebrated the event in the usual style:

> *Hark! from yonder Line the loud signal is sounding,*
> *Like the war-whoop of India, or loud battle yell;*
> *The arches reply with shrill echoes rebounding,*
> *And jarring in discord still louder they swell.*
> *'Tis the Birmingham Engine, full charged on the metal,*
> *Her sulphurous breath on the breezes she blows:*
> *Through the green vales of Craven, from Skipton to Settle,*
> *Discharging her lava, as onward she goes...*

And finally:

> *Then Alock and Sharp—of this line the projectors,*
> *With Dawson and Birkbeck as equal compeers;*
> *In bumpers we'll toast them, with all the Directors,*
> *And Britain's fair QUEEN! with the Commons and Peers.*

Come to Zion!

BY the 1840s, Zion Chapel was thriving. Among its new members were Daniel Nelson and his family, recently arrived in town. They had an early encounter with the Robinsons, who lived in grand surroundings at at Cragdale.

Mrs Robinson, being driven in her carriage along Duke Street, overtook a lady and two girls, who did not courtsey to her, as local custom demanded. The coachman took up the matter and discovered they were members of the Nelson family.

Daniel Nelson, when told about Mrs Robinson's displeasure, said: 'None of my family will bow or courtsey to anyone but our Maker.' The defiant man became a friend of the Robinsons. They admired his forthright manner and his musical abilities. Daniel was sometimes asked to take his 'cello to Cragdale and join their string quartet for the evening.

A descripton of Zion Chapel at this time was penned by the Rev Samuel Compston: 'The Chapel interior (then entered by two front doors) was extremely bare. The pews in the central area were of plain deal and of strictly 'perpendicular architecture'. The sides had forms for Sunday School purpose, the Scholars at Christmas being treated (as were the Wesleyans) to a breakfast of coffee and a bun (curran wig) at 8 a.m.

'A big iron stove occupied part of one side, but when in use the smoke and fumes were oft as rebellious to train in the way they ought to go, as naughty boys. When such incense did not prevail, an air of mustiness did, from long-existing damp.

'The vestry was within the south-east corner of the chapel: and the gallery was not used in winter. There was no matting or other covering on chapel or vestry floor, nor carpet for the pulpit stairs. Illumination in dark weather was by means of tallow dips, grouped in tens and twelves...

'There were two 'singing pews', but no instrument except a bass fiddle played from time to time by Titus Nelson. Otherwise, the tunes were 'pitched' by Dicky Isherwood, of Runley Bridge Toll-bar, or by the pastor who was a good bass singer as well as a 'cellist.

'Eventually, to aid the musical service, a harmonium was bought, the 'cello still taking its part on special occasions: and a choir was formed, much to the joy of the congregation.'

Giggleswick Fair

ON March 12, when the annual fair was held at Giggleswick, cattle as well as people thronged the main street. Their owners had brought them either for sale or exchange.

A member of the Compston family, then a scholar at Giggleswick School, which he left in 1857, recalled that 'a number of the cattle had come from lonely hillside farms, where they led placid lives accustomed to gentle treatment, especially from the female attendants; but here they were nervous and restless, some with distended udders, the barking of dogs and rustic calls adding to the agitation of both bipeds and quadrupeds.'

Giggleswick Fair coincided with Speech Day and prize distribution at Giggleswick School. 'Visitors who came primarily on account of the function at the school picked their way as best they could. Dainty shoes and dresses were very liable to become soiled, especially the expanded skirts of ladies who had begun to adopt the crinolined style of frocks...

The Ribble Bridge

'Two at least of the school governors [Chris Geldard of Capple-side and John Preston of Merebeck] were gentleman farmers who came on horseback, and while viewing the Fair assisted in the clearing of a course for disconcerted ladies along the outer edge of the crowds.'

At School, the report of the school year and notable recent advances of former pupils were set forth. Visitors were entertained to 'rhetorical or elocutionary displays in one language or another, in prose or verse, by a few of the senior forms. Then each prizeman was called, walked up to the headmaster's table, received his prize and walked down again amid general cheering.

'After a brief speech or two of congratulation and advice came the serving out to each boy of a paper containing two or three figs and a small cake. Many of the fellows did not care a fig for the figs and soon were throwing them at each other and their friends as the company dispersed.'

The *Hart's Head* and *Black Horse* did great business. Here and there a cottage had a table outside on which were sweets for sale—'peppermints, humbugs and the like, or pies, tripe, small beer and pop and other refreshment.'

New Faces

SETTLE was scarcely a deep-died Yorkshire community. The Census of 1851 reveals an astonishingly large number of 'heads of household' born over 10 miles from the town.

Of the 67 people in this category, four had come from Scotland, six from Ireland, one from Wales, 11 from other parts of Yorkshire, 25 from Lancashire and 20 from other English counties.

The Vicar was from Hitchin and the minister at Zion hailed from Oswestry. The Lancashire contingent included two cotton manufacturers and some of their workpeople. A farm steward came from Scotland.

The most intriguing entry concerned Nancy Smith, a visitor staying in Eagle Yard. At the time the Census was taken, this 34 year old Irish woman was 'gone and not known'.

Village Tales

MISS Minnick, a woman of much property, was among the well-to-do attending Giggleswick Church. She had a right to one of the old box pews, which she occupied with her retainers each Sunday.

When it was proposed to replace the box pews with a type which occupied less space, Miss Minnick denounced it as vandalism, vowing that if such a thing happened she would sit in her pew day and night. She owned her pew, and she was a wealthy woman, so the task of refurbishment was left until after her death.

Tommy and Dicky Monk were members of the White Dog Club which met at a wooden seat beside the lych gate. A Club member must never possess a watch or take off his coat to work. He must always lie down when it was sunny and, should the day be hot, he must lie absolutely still until someone came to turn him over.

Tommy, who was Sexton at the Church, dressed in a frock coat which became green with age. He conducted a private war with lads who teased him by using the churchyard as a playground.

An excellent trombonist, Tommy often played with the other instrumentalists in the church. He composed a 'hymn' to mark the visit of a Bishop:

> *Now the mountains do skip,*
> *And the hills do hop,*
> *To welcome to town*
> *My Lord Bishop.*

Jimmy Howson, who lived in a cottage near the *Black Horse*, wrote some lines about the locality, his song beginning:

> *At Giggleswick Fair on the twelfth of March*
> *There you will see a few young upstarts,*
> *Running, jumping, singing and dancing*
> *Like young stags that's fond of prancing.*

No great work of literature was penned at Giggleswick, though Mrs G Linnaeus Banks made Ivy Fold, near the Church, the setting of her 'healthy' story, entitled *Wooers and Winners; or Under the Scars.*

The Monk family were among the last of the handloom weavers who worked in the top room at Armistead House. The windows were generally filled with canary cages for breeding purposes. They taught the young birds to whistle by imitation.

Miss Mary Waller, tall and spare, one of the daughters of the family at the *Black Horse,* had a private school for girls and young ladies of from 16 years of age. The school was held in the upper room of an out-building.

Vile Smell of Gas

SETTLE was lit at night by vegetable gas, produced by Mr Hassel, a Hull man whose gasworks were on Bond Lane. The gas 'smelled most viley'. After making as much gas as he thought the local people would require [at a charge of 12s per thousand feet] the gasman locked up and went home.

The stench from vegetable gas was so bad there was general rejoicing when, in 1856, Settle was supplied with coal gas by a company in which John Tatham, a prominent local businessman, was involved.

A gasometer was erected in the yard near the Victoria Hall. Local lads, trespassing in a neighbouring garden, hurled heavy sods on it which resounded and brought out an indignant attendant, known as Tommy Gas.

When the gasworks were moved to Upper Settle, the tar-water was turned into a drain which discharged it into the river. All the fish were poisoned. Jacky Moorby was fishing at the time and, having a net, he raked in the stupified trout by the dozen.

These were tastefully decked out in a basket and, as there was to be a dinner party at Beck House that night, several pounds were purchased. When the guests sat down to eat the fish, they were surprised at the extraordinary flavour.

A New School

IN 1856, the two Settle schools—one for boys, the other for girls—were amalgamated and the joint enterprise moved to its present site on the slopes of Castleberg.

John Robinson, grandson of John Peart, exchanged the northern end of Mrs Birkbeck's field in Upper Settle for the Old School. Assisted by his father, William Robinson, and several friends, he built two commodious Schoolrooms, a classroom and a Master's House.

Passing Through

QUEEN Caroline's coach stopped briefly at the *Golden Lion*. Friends of Jimmy Carr bet him the price of a pint he would not dare to speak to her. Jimmy rushed up and put his hand in at the coach window.

Queen Caroline could do little else but take the hand, whereupon Jimmy is reported to have said: 'Eh! God bless you ma'm. What a nice lile soft white hand ye hev.'

'Little' North Western

THE Trustees of the Keighley-Kendal Turnpike, meeting in 1849, discussed the close proximity of the new railway to the Turnpike and concluded 'there is danger to the passengers on the road from Skirbeck to Mr Preston's gate at Mearbeck because of horses being frightened by the sight of engines'.

The canny trustees sent notice expressing this concern to the railway company and thus absolved themselves from responsibility for accidents. Subsequently a solid wooden fence was erected between the railway and the road so that horses could not see a passing train.

Giggleswick station being unhandy to Settle, Parliamentary authority was obtained 'to make a new road, to commence at or near Beggarwaith Bridge otherwise Beggarwife Bridge, in the Township of Giggleswick, and to terminate at or in the Town of Settle'.

The company bought the *New Inn,* on Duke Street, the new road cutting through what had been the inn yard to join an existing road [Goldielands] near the Lodge serving Ashfield. With Goldielands widened and improved there remained the task of making a road directly to Four Lane Ends and the station.

The Ribble was spanned by a cast iron bridge, subsequently known as the Penny Bridge because of a modest toll payable by those who used it. Anyone who subscribed towards the cost of the bridge was permitted to cross free of charge.

The railway undoubtedly affected the revenue of the Turnpike trustees by diverting freight from the road, which was still being maintained to a high standard. In the 1850s, a stone-breaker preparing material for the Turnpike found himself with a considerable number of large calliards [stones without grain] which were unbreakable.

When some schoolboys inquired about the calliards, the stone breaker said: 'Them's swimming stones. If ye tak 'em down to Ribble and throw 'em in, you'll see for yoursels.'

Each boy carried a heavy stone down to Birkbeck Weir, where

the stones sank without trace. Not to be outdone, the lads mentioned the 'swimming stones' to their friends. So the old stone breaker got all his calliards cleared away.

Music and Drama

GIGGLESWICK Church had a loft in front of the belfry 'where the village musicians, vocal and instrumental, used to give of their best.' At other times, Billy Guyer accompanied the choir on a bass fiddle. Two calf-skin covered drums were used in the days before an organ was installed.

John Hare (later, Sir John Hare, the celebrated actor) knew the district well, having boarded at Giggleswick when he was a boy. He was recalled as 'a handsome dark lad, who appeared at our penny readings.' He played in burlesque at the Mechanics' Hall, which became the Liberal Club.

About 1860, Messrs Barnett and Stansfield, having just returned from the Conservatoire of Music, in Leipsig, organised an orchestra. The folk of Settle had their first taste of theatrical venture on a grand scale. The proceeds went towards the Lancashire textile workers who were suffering during the great cotton famine.

An operatic society began in the 1870s, when—the Settle-Carlisle Railway having been opened—some patrons of the art found the train times inconvenient for attending shows in Leeds or Bradford. They decided to produce some shows for themselves and for many years the works of Gilbert and Sullivan entranced patrons at the Victoria Hall.

Christies at Langcliffe

IN 1861, Mr Lorenzo Christie, who had mills at Edale in Derbyshire, purchased the Clayton cotton mill at Langcliffe. The mill had been closed through trade recession. Christie built Shed Mill as a weaving shop.

Then, needing workers, Christie brought the first recruits from Devonshire and East Anglia.

The business was carried on by his son, Hector, who recalled the good work done at the Derbyshire mills by Henry Brassington and consequently invited him to move to Settle with his wife and family.

The Christies built houses at Langcliffe for their workers. Cornish families sustained the local Chapel. The Christie family were pillars of the Church and built the Langcliffe Institute. High Mill and Shed had their own well-organised sports facilities, including tennis courts and bowling green.

Pioneer Co-operators

LANGCLIFFE Co-op, founded in 1829 [the first in the country] was re-established in 1861. Most of the early societies failed through lack of capital and the method of returning the profits on members' share capital.

The Rochdale Pioneers [15 years after Langcliffe's first abortive effort] evolved a successful scheme. This had an open membership, gave the members a right to determine policy through the principle of one man, one vote, and paid limited interest on capital. Any surplus or profit was returned to members in proportion to their purchases.

The Settle society of 1861 was based on a store in Victoria Street. Forty-five members were enrolled and the amount of paid up capital came to £93.7s. The first quarter's receipt for goods sold was £238.13s.2d. Two members looked after the store in the evening. It was eventually decided to compensate them for their trouble.

Tall Buildings

SETTLE acquired some high-rise building about the year 1870, when John Parker, of Lodge Farm, with an eye on commercial savings, had a block of dwellings constructed near the Folly at Settle.

He also built Pendle View, near the *Hart's Head* at Giggleswick, which is similarly large and high, having two houses, with flats below. The flats were in an area fronting some cellars.

G H Brown, the Zion parson, lived here for a while. Having a large family, he occupied a house, two adjoining flats and the cellar.

Settle-Carlisle Railway

SETTLE acquired a railway of its own with the construction of the Settle-Carlisle (1869-1876). Documents at Langcliffe Hall provide us with an insight into the legal processes by which a railway company took over the strip of land it required for a new line.

The proposed route lay within a short distance of the 17th century hall, the home of Mrs Jane Perfect. Her estate included Barrel Sykes, which had been purchased in 1863.

On May 14, 1869, Mrs Perfect received notification that under the terms of the Midland Railway (Settle to Carlisle) Act, 1866, the Company required to purchase and take four acres, one rood and five perches of land.

W H Wood, of Colne, valued the land at £1,638.10s. He worked this out as four acres 1 rood 5 perches, at 100s an acre, adding 50 per cent to the value for 'compulsory taking'. He also took into account the depreciation of lands that were intersected by the railway (32-1-28 at 7s.6d per acre) and for depreciation of residence (30 years purchased at £5).

Mr Wood, in sending his valuation to C H Charlesworth (the solicitor acting for Mrs Perfect) added: 'It is a safe one, and one which you may rely upon being supported before anyone. Indeed, I think it would not be unreasonable to ask the Company £150 more.' (Unbeknown to Mr Wood, the Company had offered £1,750).

So a strip of land was sold. The railway's course lay a few yards from Barrel Sykes but, near Langcliffe Hall, ran in a deep cutting. Train noises were muffled.

With a large workforce in town for the building of the railway, the pubs of Settle had a lively trade. Residents winced at some of the excesses of the navvies.

In 1870 there was 'bad blood' between the English workers on the line and the relatively few Irishmen. A disturbance occurred at the *Crown,* in Settle. An English mason, having struck a foreman, Peter Quin, appeared before the magistrates and was fined 20s.

At Leeds Assizes, in April, 1871, Ellis Parker, alias Nelson, a navvy, was sent for penal servitude for five years for the manslaughter of Christopher Wright of Langcliffe.

Sophia Sidmill, alias Boxmore, was brought before the Bench charged with committing a violent assult on Richard Simmonds, a navvy. She was liberated when the Bench heard the two had 'arranged the matter between them'.

In 1872, the Settle Bench considered the case of three men playing pitch and toss on the New Road on a Sunday. In another case, they fined David Hayes, a railway labourer, 21s with costs when he pleaded guilty to damaging the door of the King William IV inn at Settle. He had drunk too much and kicked the door, the damage being estimated at 3s.

John Griffith Owen, of Holyhead, killed by the fall of a crane in Langcliffe Cutting, was buried in Settle churchyard with an inscribed stone to mark the spot. Tom Twistleton, the Craven Bard, wrote a poem about his death and a fellow Welshman arranged for the gravestone to be inscribed:

> *Ai mewn bedd mai Ioan bach-O I'e*
> *Ioan sy'n llwch bellach*
> *Ond daw'n ol ctto'n iach*
> *At ail vesi'n fil tlysach.*

A literal translation is:

> *Young John is now in his Grave*
> *John that is Ashes now;*
> *But he'll come back a second time*
> *A thousand times better.*

In 1873, the area of the present station was enclosed and temporary buildings erected. Here were stables, a covered building for a sawing machine and a mortar mill, the mortar being composed of lime from Leicestershire known as 'hydraulic'; it was ground by steam power and carried in trucks to the various bridges.

At Settle Music Hall, in 1873, the sum of £10 was raised by an entertainment—glees, songs, readings and recitations—for the funds of the Settle-Carlisle Railway Sick Fund. The Club, established in 1870, was reported to have 140 members.

During the following year, there was concern about the close proximity of Barrel Sykes [then the home of G W Perfect] to the route selected for the railway. 'There has only been just sufficient room to get an easy curve without pulling down the house.'

Police Superintendent Copeland, having received a number of complaints of the illicit sale of beer and spirits at Settle and Giggleswick, was determined to put a stop to it. A spokesman for the Bench said that future cases of this description 'would be severely dealt with'.

By 1876, the station at Settle Junction was complete and a close paling [fence] erected to prevent the station from being seen near the road. Settle now had a range of railway buildings, constructed of Bradford stone in the form of a double gable, separated by a central porch, with a wood and glass screen. The general style was referred to mockingly as 'Midland Gothic'.

Settle also had a goods warehouse to accommodate five trucks at once. Other facilities were cattle pens, signal box and water cranes. Six cottages were provided for signalmen and porters.

A *Craven Herald* reporter mentioned complaints he had heard about the poor arrangements for goods and cattle traffic. Both had been formed 'without the slightest regard for their easy working.' The entrance to the booking office is also planned as awkwardly as it well could be, being out of sight, round a corner, and nothing to guide a stranger to its whereabouts. The simple removal of the door on the opposite side would remedy this defect at small cost.'

F S Williams, historian of the Midland Company, called here in 1876 and saw 'the pretty passenger station, built of freestone...'

Local Tycoons

WHEN the first goods trains were rattling along the Settle-Carlisle railway, in 1876, Messrs Wilson and Clarke, who had made a fortune out of lime-burning, arranged for a Hoffman's kiln, three times the size of the one they had installed at Mealbank, Ingleton, to be built at a site near the railway at Craven Quarry, Langcliffe.

The quarry was developed by the newly-established [1873] Craven Lime Company Ltd. [Wilson, a half-forgotten tycoon, died on April 2, 1891, aged 74, and was interred at Clapham].

Meanwhile, young John Delaney found a mission in life—quarrying limestone. He literally made a mark on the district at his Beecroft Quarry at Horton-in-Ribblesdale.

Delaney was born in Ireland in 1846 [the Hungry Forties, when the potato blight was at its worst]. His father, agent for an absentee landlord, had to collect rents from starving tenants. One night, as he rode home, he was shot dead by Moonlighters [rebellious small-holders].

His eldest daughter, Ann, settled the family at Stalybridge in Cheshire. Some of the children moved into Norfolk, but John Delaney went to Settle, to work in the mill of Hector Christie, where he became an Overseer.

John Delaney

Delaney married Annie Calvert, a Lancashire weaver, and they settled in Langcliffe. The next ten years were a grim struggle for economic survival, and only then did Annie get her engagement ring. Two daughters were born, one dying in infancy.

Delaney found that the job at Christie's mill was not sufficient to occupy his energies and ideas. He began to trade in his spare time and when the Settle-Carlisle railway was opened for freight traffic, he concentrated on coal.

Needing £40 to buy a horse and cart, and finding the local banks would not advance him the money, he received money, guidance and friendship from an old Quaker banker in Sheffield. He became a Quaker, with strong convictions.

At Christies' mill, he was given an ultimatum: to work here or leave and develop his own business interests. He departed, bought a small store in Langcliffe, left his wife to run it and care for their surviving daughter, Carrie, and went to Manchester University to study geology, having become aware of the vast reserves of almost pure limestone in North Ribblesdale.

His fortune was made by bringing in coal on railway wagons which bore his name in large letters and using those same wagons to take out the limestone to the steel mills of Sheffield, where his Quaker friends lived.

[In the 1890s, the family moved from Langcliffe to Overdale, Settle, which he had built. Delaney was still in his fifties. He died in 1921].

Hector Christie's mills were highly successful. He imported workers from Cornwall as textile operatives.

Christie wrote to William Pryor, Four Lanes, Redruth, in July, 1877. Pryor was happy for his wife and children to travel to Yorkshire for work, but he himself would remain in his native county.

Christie mentioned the working conditions. It would be a five and a-half day week, with half an hour for breakfast and one hour for dinner. On Saturday, the children would begin work at 6 a.m. and leave off at 1 p.m., 'with an interval of half an hour for breakfast only.'

Pryer was informed that the expensive of removing his five children—Mary (aged 19), Lavinia Ellen (17), Elizabeth Jane (15), Emily Grace (13) and Melendia (11)—would be covered by the mill 'but the expense of removal of your wife and any other member of your family you would have to pay yourself.

'I should however be willing to advance you the money, to be repaid by instalments of not less than 2s a week out of your children's wages. I have only one house empty, the rent of which is 4s.6d a week.' [The maximum wage for a girl was 7s a week].

In a second letter, written in August, Christie's manager acknowledged the receipt of indentures for four younger girls from a Mr Wilson and was disappointed to find that his [Mr Pryor's] daughter Mary was not coming at present. 'I believe she will yet decide to come with the other portion of your family.'

The journey from Cornwall to Ribblesdale would take two days. Christie arranged for tea, bed and breakfast to be provided for them all at Bristol.

Turnpike Trustees

A LITTLE known event of 1877 was the winding up of the Keighley-Kendal Turnpike Trust. Income from tolls had scarcely kept pace with the repairs necessary with heavier traffic. The wheels of mail coaches shredded the unmetalled road but the owners of such vehicles paid no toll.

With the coming of rail travel, the income from tolls fell. Most of those who had advanced money were losers. For example, Robert Ingleby of Lawkland received £600 for the £1,000 invested, Joseph Birkbeck of Anley £600 (£1,100) and the Farrers of Clapham £850 (£2,000).

Counting Heads

THE Census of 1881 reveals that 134 'heads' of the Settle households were born more than 10 miles from the town.

A schoolmistress had come from San Domingo. Twenty people arrived from other parts of Yorkshire, 32 from Lancashire and 69 from other English counties, representing a considerable change over the previous 30 years. Into Settle came 'offcomers' taking up railway work. And, as related, Cornish folk arrived to work at the mills.

Among those who came from a distance to take over responsible positions were the District Auditor, the Postmaster (who was also the Registrar of Births, Marriages and Deaths), the Sanitary Inspector and the manager of the Co-op, the Police Sergeant and Constable, the Inspector of the Telegraph service and a Professor of Chemistry and Physics.

The Inland Revenue Officer hailed from Ireland. William Walker, chemist and druggist, came from Rye in Sussex.

The largest lodging house, in Upper Settle, was being kept by Jane Etherington, an Irishwoman, wife of a railway porter who had been born in Settle. In addition to her own fairly numerous family, Jane had 24 adult lodgers, including eight Irishmen, and several of their children.

Another lodging house was catering for five Irishmen, three of whom were pedlars, another being a labourer and the fifth a cotton operative. A railway signalman from Northants had three lodgers who were railway porters, hailing from Wales, Durham and Hull.

High Society

THE social round at Settle in the 1880s included lectures for the people at the Music Hall and the Yeomanry Ball. In 1886, the menu consisted of:

Joints—Roast Ribs of Beef. Roast Lamb.
Poultry—Boiled Turkey, Roast Turkey,
Boned Turkey. Roast Chickens, Boiled Chickens.
Also
Ham and Tongue or Game Pie.
Sweets—Mince Pies, Lemon Cheese Cakes,
Vanilla Creams, Lemon Creams, Merangues,
Tipsy Cake, Wine Jellies, Trifle.

The pillars of the local society, as evidence by the officials of the North Craven Horticultural Society, were Walter Morrison, Hector Christie, Captain Stackhouse, John Birkbeck, T F Knowles, Thomas Proctor, Rev Jackson Mason, C H Charlesworth, John Roberts, W L Christie and J G Robinson.

Devil in Suspension

DEMON Drink was a scourge in Victorian Settle. In February, 1883, the Settle Gospel Temperance Union held a week-long mission, when over 1,000 people put on the blue ribbon, nearly 450 of these being new pledges.

A series of meetings, mainly for the 'industrial population' followed. Funds were raised by a Sale of Work. Mrs John Birkbeck, jnr., opened the sale which raised £72. Packed meetings were held in the Music Hall through the winter.

Snow Castle

THE winter of 1886, when the district was icebound for 16 weeks, was given a dash of magic with the creation of a Snow Castle on the Green in Upper Settle.

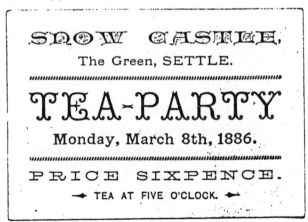

SNOW CASTLE,
The Green, SETTLE.

TEA-PARTY
Monday, March 8th, 1886.

PRICE SIXPENCE.
→ TEA AT FIVE O'CLOCK. ←

After a particularly heavy snowfall, small boys made a castle-like structure, which was enlarged and elaborated by the men until the Castle was 40 yards in circumference and 15 feet high. It boasted several turrets, from which flew Union Jacks. Inside were three large rooms, which 'were illuminated and decorated, the effect being striking and unique.'

Subscriptions were raised and refreshments supplied at wooden tables. Sixty children at a time sat down to eat and drink and eventually some 700 had partaken. Then the general public were admitted and it was reckoned that some 2,000 entered the castle, one man riding through the rooms on a donkey.

The Shambles

A BUILDING company bought The Shambles on September 19, 1887, the price paid being £1,210.

The shareholders were Hector Christie, manufacturer; Thomas Brayshaw, solicitor; Charles William Buck, surgeon; John Handby, plumber; John William Shepherd, Pharmaceutical Chemist; John Lord, grocer; and Charles John Lord, solicitor's clerk, who was appointed secretary at a salary of £5.5s.

The Shambles, a dominant structure in the town, was surmounted by a row of single storey cottages which were now given an extra storey at a cost of £674.lls.5d, 'less the sale of old timber'.

At the Workhouse

FOR the Christmas Party of 1863 [which took place on January 5, 1864] the inmates had a programme of religious and sentimental songs and poems, beginning with a hymn *Once in a Lowly Manger* and ending with *O so Bright*, followed by *God Save the Queen*.

The food normally served to the 'respective classes' was stodge, woefully deficient in fruit and vegetables. On offer [1891] was pea soup, broth, ordinary porridge, rice porridge and flour porridge; hash [Irish stew], tea, coffee or cocoa.

But mainly it was porridge that filled the stomachs of the inmates. This porridge was made with oatmeal and blue [skimmed] milk. A special treat consisted of rice, blue milk and some treacle.

Into the hash went raw meat, without bone; potato; onions; seasoning; water or meat liquor.

Tramps, also known as 'the gentlemen of the road', might be seen congregating round the bottom of Buck's Lane at Giggleswick, waiting for 6 p.m., the time when they were admitted to the Workhouse. The presence of so many strange men could be frightening to children living in the area who, in winter, had to make their way home along the side of Tems Beck in the evening gloom.

A few men, knowing that they would have to declare any money to the Workhouse authorities, surreptitiously hid it in the walls along Buck's Lane, intending to recover the cash when they vacated the Workhouse on the following morning.

Administrative Centre

THE District Councils were brought into being under the Local Government Act of 1894. On June 15, just prior to the Act becoming law, ratepayers met under the chairmanship of Hector Christie, the County Councillor.

After discussion, a resolution was approved to be forwarded in the hope of securing far better representation for Settle on a new District Council than the town had on the old Board of Guardians. This was eventually granted, but some electors still regarded the Council as a Farmers' Club. A non-farming councillor was heard to say: 'I caw that nowt but a talking shop.'

Settle Town Hall was now distinguished as the meeting place of a Council concerned with an area the size of the Isle of Man. In town was a County Court and also the headquarters of a Petty-Sessional Division. The Board of Guardians in the Settle Union, which concerned itself with the welfare of the poor, met in the same chamber as the new District Council.

Politically, Settle and Giggleswick gave strong support to the Liberals. At the election of 1895 their candidate was James Anson Farrer, of Ingleborough Hall, Clapham. From the flatbed press of J W Lambert came some election songs, set to familiar tunes:

> *Should auld acquaintance be forgot,*
> *None better can we find;*
> *This time it's Farrer we shall send,*
> *For the days of auld lang syne.*

The Liberal March used the music of 'Men of Harlech':

> *Men and Liberals! rouse to action,*
> *Never let a Tory faction*
> *In your ranks spread wild distraction!*
> *Hark! the trumpet's call!*

Market Day

SETTLE on a Tuesday, Market Day, was thronged with farming folk. Every spare yard of ground was filled with horses and traps.

In season, an 'entire' [uncastrated stallion] was brought into town to sire the farmers' mares, one venue being the yard of the *White Horse,* on the north-western side of the market. In 1895, Colonel Foster, of Hornby Castle, made available Lord Montebegon, his fully registered Hackney stallion.

Market Day usually filled the local hostelries, though in 1897 the Ashfield surrendered its licence for the sale of intoxicating drinks—and thus lost some of its popularity. The hotel had come

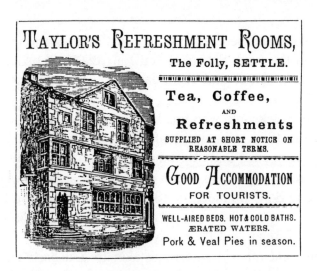
into the hands of the Rev William John Birkbeck, whose grand-father, William Birkbeck, built the place early in the century.

The new owner was a staunch teetotaller. To him, strong drink was the Devil in Suspension. He bequeathed the property to his nephew, Lawrence Henry Badock, with the stipulation that he should take the name of Carr Birkbeck (the Reverend's mother having been a Carr) and that if a licence was applied for in respect of the house, the property must be sold and the proceeds given to Settle Church.

[After being a temperance hotel for many years, the Ashfield regained its licence at the expense of the *White Horse,* the licence being transferred].

A Victorian Family

AMONG the upstanding and much respected townsfolk were the Brockbanks. They represented some of the qualities which were popularly associated with the Victorian middle-class—honesty (they were Quakers), self-reliance (Ellwood Brockbank was engaged in commerce) and a delight in novelty (he devised a pioneer method of postal shopping).

The Brockbanks believed in service to others (he was one of the founders of the Adult School at Settle in 1860) and had a love of art (his wife, Marie, and their daughter Elisabeth excelled as artists).

Ellwood Brockbank, who was born in Salford in 1841, arrived in Settle in 1856, nine years after the 'Little' North Western Railway was opened and at a time of industrial recession.

Brockbank was lucky to obtain employment at Settle with John Tatham and Sons [founded in 1816]. John Tatham and his wife Susannah were Quakers. So were their two sons, Joseph and Richard E Tatham and their sister.

This firm maintained something akin to a department store. Here were sold, in addition to groceries, drugs and chemicals, hosiery and drapery, also Bibles (being a depot of the British and Foreign Bible Society).

The firm specialised in Yorkshire hams and bacon which were fed and cured locally; also Wensleydale cheeses, weighing between one and a-half pounds and fifteen pounds; Beech's jams and jellies, evaporated apricots, peaches and pears.

Ellwood Brockbank took on an increasing responsibility in the firm and, in separate premises, he pioneered shopping by post under the title 'Fireside Shopping'. It was possibly the first mail order business in Britain or America.

His system was based on 'cash with order without discount.' Goods were supplied direct by return carriage or postage was paid to anywhere within the United Kingdom.

A trade paper of the 1880s stated that Brockbank was 'the inaugurator of a useful system for the distribution of goods at wholesale prices to retail customers throughout the country.

'A lady living in some rural district can furnish her household with dress materials, linens, blankets and various other goods by sending a line to Mr Brockbank. His goods are by the best makers and are very cheap, considering the excellence of their quality.'

Council Matters

SETTLE Rural District Council, in August, 1896, pondered on the Waterworks. The supply was then equal to 26 gallons per head per 24 hours 'but in consequence of the great waste and misuse of water, it has been found necessary to turn off the water for six hours each night.'

Anyone who, being supplied with water, 'wilfully or negligently causes or suffers any pipe, valve, cock, cistern, bath, soilpan, water closet or other apparatus or receptable to be out of repair' might be fined.

In April, 1898, the Council discussed sewers and sewage. Thomas Harger mentioned defective sewers (laid a few years before at great cost) and the 'wretched mis-management' which had let slip an opportunity for the town to secure its own gasworks (at reasonable cost).

A School Chapel

DURING the period 1897-1901, the skyline of Settle and Giggleswick was changed forever by the construction, on a prominent gritstone knoll, of Mr Morrison's domed chapel, a gift to Giggleswick School in the Diamond Jubilee year of Queen Victoria.

An old man wanted to know why the School should want a 'heathen temple' on the hill when there was a perfectly good church in the village.

The chapel was designed by T G Jackson, a leading architect, whose commission was to put a dome on a gothic building. This expression of the Christian Faith in the confident style of High Victorianism was finished and furnished in a single furious building spree. Morrison did not want to leave any scope for additions, which might be unsympathetic to his grand idea.

The dome was constructed by a novel method, with interlocking blocks of terracotta. The outside was of timber, covered with copper. Inside was glass mosaic, with sixteen angels, each over six feet high, playing musical instruments and the seated figures of the evangelists with their respective emblems.

The main walls were created of local gritstone, faced externally with yellow Idle [Bradford] sandstone up to the plinth. Commemorated in stained glass are Edward VI [copied from an illumination on his original charter], James Carr [founder], the Rev George Style [Headmaster at the time of the chapel's construction] and, of course, Morrison himself, looking pleased as he holds a model of his chapel.

A New Century

IN February, 1899, the Duke of Devonshire, having inherited the market rights from his forebears, granted them to Settle Parish Council, providing that the Council 'keeps the Market Place in repair and does not build on it anything except a urinal.'

Settle magistrates fined James Harrison, of Paythorne, 7s.6d and costs for being drunk while in charge of a horse, and John Beattie of Long Preston 2s.6d and costs for being asleep while in charge of a horse and cart. Mr Atkinson's carriage and a farmer's trap collided near Settle Bridge.

The Rural District Council applied to the Local Government Board for sanction to borrow £4,699 for sewage works in the townships of Giggleswick, Langcliffe and Settle.

There was much news about the Boer War. In March, Carrie Delaney, secretary of the Women's Liberal Association, received a letter from Mrs Kitchener, wife of Col. Kitchener, thanking them for a box of shirts which 'I am giving to the men whose shirts have gone to pieces.'

On June 1, rejoicing greeted the news of the Relief of Mafeking. Bands played and Church services were packed.

Summer attractions included cheap excursions on the Midland Railway 'every Saturday during July to Morecambe (from Giggleswick) and from Skipton through the Lake District to the Isle of Man. The picturesque and short sea route, via Barrow (passage 3 hours). Train from Skipton at 12-5 noon connects with the daily service by the magnificent Express steamer *Duchess of Devonshire* and other first-class paddle steamers.'

The Volunteer Movement, which began in 1859, had Walter Morrison as Colonel and met at the Drill Hall, against Castleberg. On December 21, 1900, the building held 'eighty-five men and eight cyclists'.

When Peace celebrations took place to mark the end of the Boer War, a dinner was held at Mr Duckett's, the *Royal William* Hotel, for the young men and apprentices.

Elsewhere, the large marquee of the Horticultural Society had been erected and about 250 people sat down to a dinner of 'old English fare' provided by some local inns. 'At one table, a carving knife and fork, with magnificent Buck horn handles, were greatly admired.'

Terraced Housing

SETTLE experienced a building boom. Large terraced houses were the thing, with living rooms of generous size, three bedrooms (one would be subsequently converted into a bathroom) and attic rooms.

From the flagstone quarry at Helwith Bridge came great pieces of 'slate', neatly sawn, to cover the ground floor and slotted together as cisterns for soft water (rain, collected by guttering and downspouts) to be used on wash-day, with much saving on soap. Local water, coming off the limestone, is hard.

Thomas Harger built Prospect Terrace. He installed three aunts in one house and his brothers moved into two others, while he himself selected a fourth house as his residence. Thomas then built the terrace known as Halsteads and, naturally, chose one of the dwellings for himself and his family.

He was a good-natured man, a stalwart Methodist much given to unpublicised good deeds. Meeting an ill-clad 'gentleman of the road', Thomas went home, changed into his best suit and gave his working suit to the tramp.

In 1907, Hector Christie, industrialist, purchased Jervaulx Abbey, with its fine house, the ruins of the monastic building and 10,000 acres of land. The previous owner had been Lord Masham.

Medical Matters

THE Settle Division of the St John Ambulance Brigade purchased, in 1908, a rapid means of transporting an ailing person—two tandems, fastened together, with a stretcher between them. Described as a cycle ambulance carriage, it cost £35.

Four men, pedalling furiously, could speedily transport any urgent medical case to the doctor or, if treatment at Skipton or Leeds was necessary, to the railway station.

In 1909, a new isolation hospital was opened at Harden Bridge, Austwick, under the auspices of the Settle Rural District Council.

Co-op Housing

THE Settle Equitable Industrial Co-operative Society, in the quarter ending March 7, 1908, paid a dividend on £1,470. In 1912, premises at Langcliffe were purchased for £160, the Craven Terrace shop at Settle having been opened in the previous year.

The year 1899 was notable for the decision to build seven houses, the following tenders being accepted: Hardy, for masons' work, £915; Russell for joiners' work, £410; Metcalfe and Stork for plastering, £220; and Hayton for plumbing, £67.

Moving Picture

IN the year 1912, Frederic Riley of Settle lectured in Zion Schoolroom on *The Ribble, from its Source to the Sea*. This included 'glimpses of the surrounding country, together with objects of Picturesque and Historic Interest along the Ribble Valley', being illustrated by 'ninety hand-coloured lantern slides from an entirely new series of original photographs.'

Isaac Hartley, of Nelson, lectured on *Tramps in the Ingleborough District*, 'being a series of outings in the land of waterfalls and subterranean passages'. Cuthbert Hastings, a pioneer potholer, lectured ('with lantern slides') on the Ingleborough potholes.

It was the heyday of 'magic lanterns', soon to be followed by 'moving pictures'.

Settle's first cinema was established in the Craven Assembly Rooms in 1912 by Robert Dale, who called his enterprise 'The Picture House'. For the first 18 months the 'pictures' were well

Victoria Hall, Settle (courtesy of the Operatic Society)

supported, but in the spring of 1914 the receipts (as was usual in hot weather) fell away. Mr Dale closed down for the summer and the cinema did not open again under his management.

The owners of the Assembly Rooms brought in R Haworth from Leeds, who was in turn succeeded by Tanny (Nathaniel) Jerome, a man of German extraction who does not appear to have his nationality held against him in the heightened emotional years of the Great War.

The silent films had piano accompaniment. Sometimes a trio was present, with Olive Marson on the piano, Arthur Horner playing the 'cello and Jim Haygarth as violinist.

Settle Personalities

HAROLD Umpleby (1915) summed up Settle as: 'Quiet but important agricultural centre. No cattle marts. Seasonal fairs. Little Motor Traffic, thanks to Buckhaw Brow.'

He recalled some of the characters, including Miss Wilkinson Newsholme (Miss Wilks) who was the book-keeper at Tathams and, as such, had the last word in efficiency. Auditors simply could not find any mistakes in her books, yet she must have been 70 years old when she retired.

Police Sergeant Wright knew how to put every ounce of dignity into a sergeant's movements. To see him heading the annual Band of Hope procession was a sight to remember. Woe betide anything that got in the way.

And there was Old Starkie of Ribble Terrace. He was a scrounger and miser—a wealthy man posing as almost destitute. A common sight was to see him with his miserable half starved dog, a piece of string fashioned to its collar because he could not afford a dog lead.

Occasionally, he would ask people to store boxes for him; they agreed. After his death, his belongings were gathered in as various people notified the exor of boxes in store. Most of those boxes were full of unused goods—household linen, cutlery, crockery. Huge chests of silver and cut glass were stored at the Banks. The Exors hired the Victoria Hall for a week for the sale.

The War Years

AS war clouds gathered in 1914, rumours about the enemy abounded. It was said [wrongly] that the Catholic priest was a spy who used the large outdoor cross, which was faced with mirror glass to reflect the evening light, as a device for signalling to the enemy.

[Fr Tilman was indeed German by birth. He was wrongly interned during the war and with the compensation he received, he bought a plot of land where, today, stands the new Catholic Church].

In 1914, the Territorials left Settle for Skipton, prior to being transferred to the East Coast. They received gifts of tobacco, bought with the proceeds of a brass band concert in the Market Place.

At Settle was raised Mr H G Tunstill's Company of Kitchener's Army; they had departed from the town to the strains of the National Anthem, the detonation of railway fog signals and amid a fluttering of handkerchiefs. Not many returned.

The handsome young sons of the Stackhouse and Birkbeck families were among the first men from the Craven district to be killed in the war. Captain W T Stackhouse, of the Sherwood Foresters, was only 32 years old. Three months later, his brother, Second Lieut J H Stackhouse, was wounded at the Front.

Settle Board of Guardians arranged for margarine, not butter, to be served to the inmates of the Workhouse, the saving being £200 a year. Mr Charlesworth said that people who were now using margarine instead of butter could hardly tell the difference.

The Procter family, of Settle, suffered grievously in the 1914-18 war. James Procter was a master tailor who worked in the attic of the family house in Duke Street. He sat cross-legged on the floor in the traditional manner. He and his wife, Mary Ann, had three daughters and two sons.

Mrs Procter presided over the St John Ambulance Brigade, which owned the famous 'ambulance', consisting of two tandems, side by side, with a stretcher on a frame between them. She died during the war.

Doris Procter became a nurse and, while serving in France, contracted septicaemia. Brought back to England for treatment, she died shortly afterwards in hospital at Birmingham. Sydney Procter, who became a soldier, was killed on active service.

Straitened Times

IN the 1920s, the lamplighter made his evening tours of Settle. His claim for a 13-week supply of matches at 1s.6d a week was met by the Rural Council.

The land which was to be 'fit for heroes' fell upon lean times. The Surveyor of the Council reported that workmen whose standard wages were under £3 a week were paid overtime at the rate of 1s.3d an hour.

At a meeting of Settle Parish Council, the Clerk asked for a salary increase. Mr J W Dales did not know when 'this vicious circle [of wage demands] will be broken. Everyone who does a pennorth of work wants one penny.'

On Christmas Day, 1921, John Delaney died [from pernicious anaemia] and was interred in the Quaker burial ground at Settle. He had willed £5 to every workman in his employ.

Some of them recalled the quirky business methods of this 'stocky little fellow', such as his habit of always doubling an order for supplies ['It's a good investment']. When a worker protested at his lot and added: 'Look at my shirt; it's wet through', Delaney replied: 'My shirt is always wet!'

His daughter, Carrie, continued the business. She had little else but hard work since childhood. At one time, when the family owned the *Temperance Hotel,* in Commercial Yard, she worked as a waitress.

Eventually, she lived in style at Overdale, had an apartment in London, and travelled around in a Rolls Royce driven by Mr Barwick, her chauffeur. Those who were unfamiliar with Carrie's changed lifestyle, and who remembered her as a waitress, stared with amazement as she was driven by.

William Ingham, the 'big chief' at Langcliffe Mill, lived in some state at Langcliffe Place, formerly the home of Hector Christie.

Hector's brother, W C Christie, had fine house and a stable of good horses at Jervaulx in Wensleydale. A Settle craftsman who did work for Christie mentioned him to some scrapmen, who called to see him. They later reported that instead of discussing business, he had shown them round his stables and were given a 'certainty' for the races. The scrapmen went to the races—and lost £50.

The *Rezzi* [residential express] called at Giggleswick on its way to Bradford and collected such as William Ingham and Charles John Lord, coal merchant, en route for Manchester, via Hellifield, Frank Marlor, of Close House, went to the Wool Exchange in Bradford, with Geoffrey Dawson of Langcliffe Hall, Editor of *The Times*, returning to London after a spell on the family estate.

Tanny Jerome moved his Picture House to the Victoria Hall, where he was succeeded by John Graham. Soon the Hall echoed to the sound of gunfire in cowboy films. The 'talkies' had arrived.

The Twenties

AT the September meeting, 1920, Settle Rural District Council decided on a half yearly rate of 4s.4½ in the £. It was noted that delay had been experienced in constructing an aerial ropeway from the limeworks of P W Spencer to Giggleswick Station.

Settle had a lively and varied group of shops, with eight grocery firms, three butchers, a fish merchant, draper, four outfitters, a milliner, four sweet shops, four pubs, two fish and chip shops and no less than four bakers and confectioners.

The Postmaster, Mr Quirke, had an assistant, W Irvine, several members of the counter staff and seven postmen, maintaining three postal deliveries each weekday—morning, noon and teatime. Incoming mail arrived by train and was transported to the Post Office on a handcart. The last collection at the pillar box in the Market Place was at 10-15 p.m.

John Moore, a Settle draper, came on to the board of the group which owned the Shambles and other local properties. The death of William Firth Clark led to the appointment of Richard Moore, John's son, who was also a draper. A third draper, John Thomas Batty, of Eshton House, Giggleswick, became a director in 1927.

In the 1920s, houses in Cammock Lane were built by Tommy Davidson, each selling for about £300. The Council, after much deliberation, built houses for those who could not afford to buy property.

Marshfield Road came into being (1924-5) and at about the same time Council houses were being built in Raines Road and Bankwell Road at Giggleswick.

Ted Fidoe, of Sutcliffe House, Giggleswick—a man of Italian extraction—made a name for himself in the Settle district as a builder. He and his wife once owned the *Black Horse*. He built some houses up the Mains and at Marshfield.

The *Pennine* bus service began on Christmas Eve, 1925, when Jim Windle drove away a blue Willis Overland bus which had collected passengers from outside Dobson's chemist shop in Skipton High Street. The first bus had 14 wooden seats, covered with a type of oilcloth. Five trips to Settle took place each weekday, with four trips on a Sunday.

No tickets were issued on that first run, the timetable having been devised with the needs of Miss Bertha McKell, a schoolteacher living at Gargrave, in mind. Miss McKell had to be at school in Coniston Cold by 9 a.m.

Pennine was founded by two brothers, Arthur and Vic Simpson, who lived at Skipton. It was Arthur who chose the bright colour scheme (orange). During a visit to Leyland Motors in Lancashire to acquire three Overlands, he saw it being used on a bus run by the works' football team. The firm was asked to use the same colour for the *Pennine* fleet.

In 1925, there was so little demand for petrol that Russian Oil Products supplied fuel in barrels. A Pennine bus drank six gallons a day, the fuel costing 7½d per gallon, if 200 gallons were ordered at a time.

In the 1920s, the road to Settle was narrow, strewn with loose stones. There were flanking dykes which were a trap to the unwary.

Watching the Eclipse

ON Wednesday, June 29, 1927, a total eclipse of the sun attracted thousands of people to Giggleswick which, being on the line of totality, had been selected as a vantage point by Sir Frank Dyson, the Astronomer Royal, who was making observations for the Royal Society.

The eclipse was due to begin by 6-24 a.m. The sun had a last minute tussle with the clouds. Then it shone through. An estimated one hundred thousand people saw the eclipse from North Ribblesdale. They included rail passengers who had hastily quit the train to stand at the lineside when the *Flying Scotsman* broke a drawber and twelve special trains were held up.

In the official party were Ramsay Macdonald, William Leach (MP for Bradford), Tom Snowden, Sir James Barrie and Sir John Simon.

Education Matters

SETTLE Girls' High School, which opened in 1913 with space for about 100 girls, now held 120 pupils and had seven full-time teachers. No transport to school was provided. Pupils who lived at a distance had to use public transport or board out with vetted families in Settle.

In 1931, R N Douglas was succeeded as Headmaster of Giggleswick School by E H Partridge, an outstanding educationalist. He organised alterations to the Hostel which emphasised the separate life of the four houses and made it possible for all boys to share a study.

A preparatory department opened at Beck House soon proved to be too small and in 1934 was transferred to Catteral Hall, where 67 boarders and 22 day boys were accommodated.

In 1938, a new wing, containing studies and a dormitory, was added to Beck House to serve as a fifth house similar to those in the Hostel. This was to meet the increase in the number of boarders.

At a time of industrial slump in the North-East, young women from mining families found employment in the Settle area, many of them as domestic workers at Giggleswick School, where for a few years Finnish girls were being recruited.

Mill Days

CHRISTIES were the principal mill-owners of the district. In the 1930s, when Jack Ingham was the general manager at Langcliffe High Mill, some 250 people were on the payroll, with over 100 workers at Shed Mill.

The first buzzer sounded at 7-45 a.m. and the second buzzer—the final warning—was to be heard three minutes later. Those who did not pass through the mill gates at 7-45 had to go to the Penny Hole, where their names were recorded and a penny docked from their week's wage, which for a man was about 30s a week, a woman receiving only half that amount.

In the first week of August, the mills closed down for the annual [unpaid] holiday. Once there was a Chapel trip to Jervaulx Abbey, in Wensleydale, the home of W L Christie. Attractions near home included the mill tennis court, bowling green and putting green. In the 1930s, it was not unusual for a person to wait from two to three hours for half an hour's play.

Sunday sport was frowned upon. 'The Christie family and t'better end went to Church. The mill-workers attended Chapel, and never the twain shall meet.'

At the Big House

LIVING at Anley in the 1930s were Col. John Birkbeck and his wife, Muriel, a member of the wealthy Braithwaite family of Leeds and best remembered in the Settle area because of her support for the St John Ambulance Brigade.

The early nineteenth century mansion could still impress people by its style and spaciousness. One who worked at Anley at this time recalled in particular the sweeping staircase, with its blue carpeting and brass stair rods.

Col. John is recalled as a kindly man, except to game, which he despatched with all the verve of the country gentleman. After a few hours in the crisp outdoor air, shooting pheasants which were retrieved by Irish water spaniels, the party of about 15 men would repair to a hut in the woods for a meat and potato pie. [Col. John's ashes were scattered in his beloved woods].

The outdoor staff at Anley consisted of two gamekeepers and three gardeners. The greenhouses contained peaches, nectarines, grapes, tomatoes and cucumbers. These glasshouses ensured that the family could have roses at Christmas-time.

Inside the house were six servants—a housekeeper, cook, kitchen maid and two parlour maids. Most of the girls came from mining areas of Durham and they tended to marry local men.

The average wage was about 6s a week, with keep. The uniform provided consisted of a dark dress and white apron. When Mrs Birkbeck had a bridge party, sandwiches made of home-grown cucumbers were served.

Guardians and Councillors

DURING the 1930s, the Clerk of the Rural Council was T E Pearson, who was also a solicitor with a general practice. One who joined the staff in 1931 recalls that he was then about 65 years old, with white hair and goatee beard and moustache.

She also recalls, ruefully, that at the time she joined the Council staff a national cut in wages came into effect and she received 10s, with a further 2s.6d allowed because she was proficient in shorthand and typewriting. The average wage of a working man was between 25s and 30s.

In 1931, the Board of Guardians—administrators of the Workhouse—met in the chamber at the Town Hall which was also used by the District Council. Mr Pearson, as Clerk of the Guardians, took a stern view of any claim for money, an extreme case being the time the Guardians turned down a man with TB and a doctor's certificate. One Guardian thought he was fit for work. The man was dead within a month.

Mr Pearson was kind to his staff. He continued to work for the Council until the age of 70, and—wearied by his many jobs—he died shortly after his retirement, to be succeeded by D F Peacock in 1936.

The new Clerk followed tradition by being a solicitor who also had a private practice. With war clouds gathering, he was soon being inundated with 'bumf' from the Ministry. 'People did not think there would be a war—but there was!'

Second World War

ARTHUR Graham was one man who had confidence in the future. He had leased the Victoria Hall for showing films, the projectionist being Harold Smith. In 1939, Arthur built the *New Vic* cinema, which was the last word in comfort.

A large number of children, evacuees from Bradford, were found accommodation in the Settle area. A Langcliffe woman recalls: 'Children arrived by train with virtually nothing. . . They were not familiar with country life. We lived at Mill House. We had plum trees from which a mass of fruit was hanging. The children were mystified.

'They didn't touch a single plum—but just looked at them in wonder.'

Anyone who catered for an evacuee received eight shillings a week for their keep. Those who could not be placed in private homes were given accommodation at Mount Pleasant. A bright lad who had been attending Bradford Grammar School was found a place at Giggleswick School.

The *Falcon Hotel* was requisitioned by the RAF for those who were attending to the bomb stores dispersed along minor roads to the west. The RAF were the Brylcream boys and much in demand when dances were held in a hut at the *Falcon*. A Chapelgoer lamented: 'It was a closed book to well-brought-up girls. At times I wished the book could have been opened for me!'

The district had its own unit of the Local Defence Volunteers, LDV for short and 'Look, Duck and Vanish' by repute. The force was re-named the Home Guard. Police Sergeant Scott had special responsibility for the local ARP (Air Raid Precautions), which mustered at Craven Bank, Giggleswick, when the air raid warning (a banshee wail) was sounded. Land Girls appeared on the farms.

Giggleswick School held its end-of-term service in the School Chapel—in darkness, except for the small torch which E H Partridge, the Headmaster, used when reading passages of Scripture. Sometimes, during a raid on Manchester, the western sky reddened from the fires the German bombers had caused.

The Settle-Carlisle railway was used to the maximum by goods and troop trains. Americans dropped off 'goodies'—chewing gum, cigarettes and boxes of peanut butter. A signalman put a notice on his box, 'Rabbits and Eggs', and had a lively trade involving the footplate men who brought their trains to unofficial halts.

During the post-war labour shortage, Italian girls were recruited by Christies, who provided a hostel and arranged for the girls to be under the care of Miss Vessey, a part-time gym mistress at Settle Girls' High School.

New Estates

UNTIL well within living memory, Northfield was exactly that—a field at the north end of the town. It belonged to Barrel Sykes farm and extended to the Ribblesdale road.

In the early 1930s, Brassingtons built eight houses [Scar View] for the Fine Cotton Spinners, who had taken over the Christie enterprise at High Mill and Shed Mill. What remained of Northfield was developed for Council housing.

The Hon Mrs Dawson, of Langcliffe Hall, reached an arrangement whereby half the land would be used and the remainder left in an open state. During the war, part of Northfield was ploughed and planted with potatoes, which were sold to local people by the row, the purchasers being left to dig out what they had bought.

Building on Northfield began in 1949 and, the first scheme having been completed, the Council demanded what land was left, making it clear that if the owner did not yield a compulsory purchase order would be sought.

So Northfield estate spread itself over good quality farmland. Happily, some other parts of the Langcliffe Hall estate, notably the cricket field and that beside Bond Lane, remained under grass.

In 1947, Settle Rural District Council acquired a coat of arms. The shield symbolised the historical constitution of the district: Giggleswick market cross and the association with the de Percy and de Mowbray families.

Above the shield is the closed helm proper to civic arms, with its crest-wreath and decorative mantling in the basic natural colours of Craven—green and white. The crest shows the head of Ingleborough with a Craven heifer thereon and a white rose of York.

The motto, *Cavendo tutus adversa sperno,* means 'Protected by caution I scorn difficulties', derived from the motto of the Cavendish family.

Land now used for a Middle School was a farm run by Ted Robinson, who was succeeded by Eric Robinson and Carter Dent, the latter selling it to the education authority. Mill Close—named after King's Mill, was used by the Thornber family, who kept farmstock here.

In 1949, Settle Parish Council celebrated the 700th anniversary of the granting of the market charter.

Six years later, the cotton mills closed down. When the management of Christies offered to sell houses to their tenants, one family living at a three-bedroomed house in West View, where they had paid one shilling a week as rent—a figure which included general, water and sewage rates—was able to buy the property for £650.

At the local government re-organisation of 1974, the Rural Council was replaced by the Craven District Council, based in Skipton.

On December 2, 1988, the famous old road through Settle was down-graded and a new stretch of the A65 opened as the Settle and Giggleswick bypass (which cost £7 million).

The engineers played fast-and-loose with local topography by re-routing the River Ribble so that their new stretch of road might head, straight as a bow-shot, from near Cleatop to Rawlinshaw.

In 1086, Norman scribes had arrived in Settle as part of a national stocktaking following the Conquest. In 1992, another French invasion took place, this time at a social level. It was the 'twinning' of Settle with a French town. This time, the invasion of French folk had a peaceful context.

A memory of Giggleswick, old kilns at the Scar

Epilogue

WHEREVER you go in North Ribblesdale, you can be sure that someone has been there before you.

This brief history of Settle and Giggleswick began with a walk up the zig-zag path on Castleberg. Re-visit that famous limestone knoll for another languid view over the valley of the Ribble.

Let your eyes rest on well-known features, hopefully with a greater insight into the local history and topography. Settle Market Place is conspicuous; it straddles a major Fault line, the frontier between limestone and gritstone. The Tuesday market stalls rest on tarmac, below which is an expanse of fine glacial material.

Victorian terraces overswept the hillock known as Halsteads. New housing impinged on Cammock, the glacial drift mount which bears the scars of having been ploughed by Anglian settlers. During the 1939-45 war, the Observer Corps had a post here, reporting on air traffic.

The Castleberg Experience should not be rushed. Up there, the busy world is hushed and traffic sounds fade to a dull rumble.

The Settle-Carlisle Railway is still open to regular passenger traffic—and to 'steam specials' storming the Long Drag, as the first 22 testing miles of the line are known.

It would have pleased James Carr, chantry priest of Giggleswick, and founder of its most famous school, if he could have foreseen the rise of Settle and Giggleswick as a centre for education. The total number of pupils exceeds 1,000.

Giggleswick School, with a staff of almost two hundred, ranging from the academic staff to maintenance men, is one of the largest employers of labour in the district. Settle High School and Middle School (which are actually on the Giggleswick side of the river) draw in students from a wide area. The Primary School, in Upper Settle, continues the tradition of the old National Schools.

Settle, which evolved in isolation from large towns or industrial conurbations, retains its character as a Dales market town. Unwrecked seventeenth century buildings huddle near Castleberg and around the market place, thanks partly to a Civil Society [now the North Craven Heritage Trust], which taught us to cherish our vernacular architecture and partly to planning regulations which encourage dwellings made of native stone.

Settle's shops were many and varied. Now a high proportion of properties have become repositories for antiques or souvenirs, in response to the demands of tourists. The town is well served with branch offices of Building Societies and finance houses.

At the Creamery, where the largest building looks like a hanger for an airship, the latest techniques are employed, and a futuristic appearance has been given to the Sidings by a range of light industrial units.

On the debit side, Settle has lost its once formidable array of dignatories—its own Stationmaster, Superintendent of Police, Education Officer, District Council Clerk and Postmaster.

Gone are the fine roadside trees from Whitefriars, Ingfield and the Stackhouse road. Car parks have been landscaped. Cobbles from the riverside have made many plain corners attractive.

Young people usually have to leave their home town to find employment. Middle-aged and elderly people find in Settle and Giggleswick pleasant havens for their retirement. Dozens of old properties have been restored as dwellings for the in-comers. There is hardly a shabby building in the place.

Anley, the old home of the Birkbecks, is a nursing home, and two other residential centres cater for the elderly.

Traffic flows along the by-pass but heavy lorries still pass through the town. The Electricity Board surveys its grid-system from a helicopter. If you are unlucky as you stand on Castleberg, surveying your heritage, you will be stunned by the whine and whoosh of low-flying jet aircraft.

Appendices

A LOCAL CHRONOLOGY

1160 – Earliest record of an incumbent at Giggleswick Church.

1248 – Settle receives first market charter.

1498 – First mention of a bridge over the Ribble between Giggleswick and Settle.

1507 – Founding of Giggleswick School by James Carr.

1513 – Settle sends 34 men to Flodden Field.

1558 – Commencement of Giggleswick parish register.

1627 – John Speed, cartographer, refers to Ebbing and Flowing Well.

1651 – In the Civil War, Lambert and his troops encamp at Settle.

1663 – Date on carving of *Naked Man* at Settle.

1669 – George Fox visits Eldroth Hall, home of the Moores, and addresses a large company.

1675 – Building of The Folly at Settle. It has a clear view of open fields.

1675 – (circa) Construction of The Shambles.

1689 – (circa) Friends Meeting House opened.

1708 – Market Charter confirmed.

1734 – Building of *Spreadeagle* Hotel in Kirkgate.

1739 – First mention of a Workhouse at Settle.

1750 – (circa) Marshfield is built by Thomas Salisbury.

1753 – Opening of a Turnpike Road through Settle and Giggleswick.

1753 – New *Golden Lion* Hotel opened beside Turnpike route.

1755 – Settle acquires a ducal Lord of the Manor (Devonshire).

1760 – First mention of Wesleyan witness in the town.

1766 – John Wesley rides through Settle; he does not stop!

1769 – Thomas Gray, the poet, at Settle.

1770 – Inauguration of Settle Literary Society.

1773 – Proposal to dig a navigable canal from the Leeds-Liverpool system at Barnoldswick to Settle; was not carried out.

1776 – Birth of George Birkbeck (who would become founder of the Mechanics' Institutes).

1777 – John Wesley preaches near the Market Place, Settle.

1783 – Langcliffe High Mill adapted for cotton spinning.

1791 – Founding of Craven Bank (incorporating Birkbeck's Bank at Settle).

1793 – Government report indicates that local agricultural workers, working on a day basis, are being paid 2s or 2s.6d a day and finding their own victuals.

1794 – Paper-making begins at a former Langcliffe cotton mill.

1794 – A company of Volunteers formed at Settle.

1796 – Opening of first Wesleyan Chapel at Settle.

1800 – John Houseman notes that Settle is 'an inconsiderable market town' and Giggleswick 'now principally consists of a few genteel houses'.

1800 – (circa) Zig-zag path cut to the summit of Castleberg.

1804 – Lime quarrying well-established on Giggleswick Scar.

1810 – (circa) *Union* coach through Settle from Kendal to Leeds and London.

1816 – Building of Zion Chapel.

1818 – Opening of Craven Savings Bank.

1818 – Completion of the building of Anley by the Birkbeck family.

1823 – A toll bar is opened at Runley Bridge, south of Settle.

1824 – Proposal to light the town with gas.

1825 – King's Mill burnt down.

1826 – Marshfield is purchased by the Dawson family of Langcliffe Hall.

1830 – (circa) Drainage of Giggleswick Tarn.

1831 – Founding of Settle Mechanics' Institute.

1833 – Town Hall built on site of Tollbooth.

1833 – (circa) Building of Ashfield, in Duke Street.

1834 – Building of first part of Union Workhouse, Giggleswick.

1835 – Settle reported to have five cotton mills, employing 333 people.

1836 – Primitive Methodists established at Wapping Hall.

1837 – Building of an Anglican church at Settle.

1838 – Consecration of Settle Church.

1842 – Consecration of Anglican churches at Rathmell and Stainforth.

1842 – Building of Ingfield (now the *Falcon Manor* Hotel) by the Rev H J Swale.

1847 – Opening of the North Western Railway, with a station at Giggleswick.

1849 – Construction of Station (or New) Road by the railway company.

1851 – Consecration of Langcliffe Church.

1851 – Several properties in Kirkgate lighted with gas.

1853 – Victoria Hall built as a music hall.

1857 – Settle gas lighting greatly extended.

1859 – Twenty thousand sheep on show at the Settle October Fair.

1860 – Adult classes commence at Settle.

1861 – Lorenzo Christie buys Langcliffe Mill and brings in workers from Devonshire and eastern counties.

1863 – Fountain pillar erected in Market Place to replace earlier Market Cross.

1868 – Formation of (short-lived) Settle Mining Company.

1869 – Cutting of first sod of Settle-Carlisle railway at Anley.

1870 – Excavation of Victoria Cave (discovered 1838) by British Association.

1870 – Yorkshire Banking Company opens new premises formed out of the *Black Bull* inn and other property.

1873 – Formation of Craven Lime Company (to work Winskill Scar, Langcliffe).

1875 – Opening of Settle-Carlisle Railway for goods traffic.

1876 – Opening of Settle-Carlisle passenger service.

1880 – Craven Bank loses the privilege of issuing its own banknotes.

1883 – Opening of re-built Roman Catholic Church.

1890 (to 1892) – Restoration of Giggleswick Church.

1893 – Opening of St John's Methodist Church at Settle.

1898 – Cottages on Shambles re-built with upper storey.

1907 – Girls' High School in temporary premises at Undercliffe, Duke Street.

1909 – Opening of Primitive Methodist Chapel at Settle.

1913 – Opening of Settle Girls' High School in Overend Close.

1922 – Duke of Devonshire conveys to Settle Parish Council all rights and privileges, together with the land in the Market Place and on The Green.

1915 – Death of Hector Christie, who had succeeded his father at Langcliffe Mill.

1950 – Old Hall, Stackhouse, owned and occupied by W H Carr Birkbeck, is sold for £2,950. Hollin Hall Farm, Rathmell, is sold by auction for £7,400.

Population of Settle Township, 1801-1901

	Males	Females	Total
1801	512	624	1136
1811	524	629	1153
1821	731	777	1408
1831	780	847	1527
1841	1057	984	2041
1851	961	1015	1976
1861	746	840	1586
1871	1130	1033	2163
1881	1050	1163	2213
1891	1053	1200	2253
1901	1069	1233	2302

In 1841, 48 soldiers were billeted in the town. The fall in population in mid-century was through 'the stoppage of mills' leading to migration. The population increased as a large number of navvies arrived to help in the construction of the Settle-Carlisle Railway. The temporary population was given as 547 by an Educational Inspector who surveyed the town under the terms of the 1870 Elementary Education Act.